BOUNTIFUL GOODNESS

THOMAS À KEMPIS

Bountiful
Goodness

~

A Little Garden of Roses
&
The Valley of Lilies

Translated by
JOSEPH N. TYLENDA, S.J.

IGNATIUS PRESS   SAN FRANCISCO

Cover design by Riz Boncan Marsella

Cover photograph: istockphoto.com

© 2013 by Ignatius Press, San Francisco
All rights reserved
ISBN 978-1-58617-778-2
Library of Congress Control Number 2013931024
Printed in the United States of America ∞

Contents

Introduction 9

A Little Garden of Roses

1. On Seeking Good Companions and
   Avoiding Those Who Are Evil 21
2. On Fleeing the World and the Devil's
   Snares 24
3. On Seeking True Wisdom in God 27
4. On Struggling against Our Vices 29
5. On Acquiring the Grace of Devotion . . . 32
6. On Hearing and Reading the Divine
   Word 34
7. On Divine Consolation amid
   Tribulation 36
8. On the Joy of a Good Conscience in
   the Holy Spirit 38
9. On the Good Conduct of a Brother
   Who Is Humble 41
10. On the Instability of the Human
    Heart 45
11. On Having Trust in God in Difficult
    Times 48

12. On the Power of Prayer and the
    Usefulness of Pious Reading 51
13. On the Praise of Charity and Its
    Fruits 57
14. On Watchfulness and Combating
    Temptations 62
15. On Bearing One Another's Burdens 64
16. On Loving Christ and Despising the
    World 68
17. On Imitating Our Lord Jesus Christ's
    Most Holy Life 73
18. On the Eternal Praise of God 78

The Valley of Lilies

Preface 87

1. On the Three States of Human Life 89
2. On Praising God in Poverty 92
3. On the Devout Being Proven in
   Adversity 94
4. On the True Lover of God 96
5. On the Soul's Gratitude for Every
   Good Thing 98
6. On the Devout Soul's Conformity to
   Jesus Crucified 100
7. On the Pure Soul's Walking with
   God 102
8. On Peace of Heart and Finding Rest
   in God 104

9. On Recollecting One's Heart in God 106

10. On Watchfulness and Prayer against Temptation 108

11. On Fear of Eternal Punishment as a Remedy against the Vices of the Flesh . . 111

12. On Remembering Our Lord's Passion as a Remedy against Dissipation 113

13. On Calling upon the Holy Name of Jesus and That of the Blessed Virgin Mary, His Mother 116

14. On Steadfast Struggling against Vices after the Example of the Saints 120

15. On Monastic Stability 123

16. On Divine Comfort after Suffering Tribulation for the Sake of Christ 125

17. On Guarding the Heart at All Times and in All Places 128

18. On Silence and Solitude 132

19. On the Refuge of the Poor 138

20. On the Poor and Sick Lazarus 142

21. On the Clear Understanding of Holy Scripture 145

22. On the Great Merit Had from Suffering Patiently for Christ 150

23. On the Good Conversation of the Humble Monk 152

24. On Prudent Speech and Fraternal Compassion 154

25. On the Uncertainty of the Hour of Death
    and the Quick End to This Life 158
26. On the Eternal Praise of God and the
    Desire for Eternal Glory 163
27. On Praising the Holy Angels in
    Heaven 167
28. A Prayer of a Devout Lover of God . . . 170
29. On Union of Heart with God 172
30. On True Peace to Be Found in God
    Alone 175
31. On Directing the Right Intention
    to God 178
32. The Prayer of a Humble and Contrite
    Heart 181
33. On Holy Fellowship with Jesus and
    His Saints 183
34. On Placing Our Supreme Good and
    Final End in God Alone 189

Introduction

The author of both these short treatises, *A Little Garden of Roses* and *The Valley of Lilies*, is Thomas à Kempis, who is likewise the author of *The Imitation of Christ*, the most famous and most beloved Christian devotional book ever written. Though these treatises have not enjoyed the popularity of the *Imitation*, nevertheless, they stand immediately at its side by reason of their spiritual teaching. The simplicity and piety that the reader has already come to know in the *Imitation* will also be found in these. In content and style, the treatises and the *Imitation* are very similar, for the aim of all of Thomas' work is to draw the reader to a closer union with the Lord Jesus. Though similar, they are at the same time different; while the *Imitation* sets forth the basic principles of the spiritual life, these treatises have a more practical aim, that is, they treat of the virtues that one must live in order to advance in the spiritual life and that are necessary for salvation. The author's main intent here, then, is to offer the reader wise counsel and practical hints toward holiness. Much of what he says is expressed so succinctly that the text often takes on the form of a maxim.

From Thomas' pen came some three dozen devotional works, the more important ones among them, in addition to our two, are: *The Soliloquy of the Soul*, the author's personal colloquies with the Lord and counsels for leading the soul to grace; *On the Three Tabernacles*, considerations on poverty, humility, and patience; *Prayers and Meditations on the Life of Christ*, reflections on our Lord's public life, Passion, Resurrection, and Ascension; *The Elevation of the Mind*; *On Solitude and Silence*; and *Sermons to Novices*.

The Author

Thomas à Kempis was born in Germany in the small town of Kempen, near Düsseldorf, north of Cologne, toward the end of 1379 or in the early part of 1380. The family name was Hemerken; his father, John, was a blacksmith, and his mother, Gertrude, the town's schoolmistress. Hence, it was under his mother's tutelage that Thomas had his first years of schooling. In 1392, when he was entering his teens and ready for further studies, Thomas was sent to Deventer, in the Low Countries, to be trained under the Brethren of the Common Life. In going there, Thomas was following in the footsteps of his older brother, John (1365–1432), who had gone to study with the Brethren some twelve years previously.

At the time of Thomas' arrival in Deventer, brother John was no longer there; he had some years earlier joined the Brethren of the Common Life and since 1390 had been a canon at their Windesheim monastery, about twenty miles north of Deventer. So it was to Windesheim that Thomas went to meet his brother. On leaving him, Thomas carried with him his brother's letter of recommendation to Florentius Radewyns (ca. 1350–1400), Master of the Brethren in Deventer.

Master Radewyns had been one of the first disciples of Master Geert Groote (1340–1384), founder of the Brethren and of the religious movement known as *Devotio Moderna* (New Devotion). Because the spiritual life of the fourteenth-century faithful in the Low Countries was on the wane, with the people growing slovenly in the practice of their Catholic faith, Master Groote intended, by his preaching, to renew in the hearts of his hearers the faith that the Dutch had formerly had. This renewal movement came to be known as *Devotio Moderna*, though there was nothing new or novel about it. It was basically a vibrant revitalization of the faith, and so successful was this movement, involving both laity and clergy, that its followers, known as Brethren of the Common Life, soon began to operate schools that in time became the best in the Netherlands. The one in Deventer was their flagship. After Master Groote's death in 1384, Radewyns succeeded him as head of the movement and superior of the Deventer Brethren. The brother's letter thus placed Thomas under Master Radewyns' direct supervision.

Thomas spent the next seven years with the Brethren in Deventer, studying the usual subjects in which any educated person of that period was expected to be proficient, such as Latin and Greek, mathematics, history, philosophy, and religion. Inasmuch as Thomas, a resident student, lived under the close supervision of the Brethren, he likewise received a firm foundation in the Catholic faith, was introduced to the writings of the Fathers of the Church, and participated in many of the Brethren's religious devotions and practices.

When Thomas completed his Deventer studies in 1399, he went, following Master Radewyns' suggestion, to visit his brother, who since early 1399 had been prior of the newly founded monastery of Canons Regular of Saint Augustine at Mount Saint Agnes, near Zwolle. In view of Thomas' past seven-year association with the Brethren and his familiarity with their manner of life and spirituality, it was perhaps expected that Thomas would request admission into his brother's religious community. This Thomas did, and in the summer of that year, 1399, he was accepted as a candidate. Following monastic custom, he who had been known up to this time as Thomas of Kempen was now to be known, according to Latin usage, as Thomas à

Kempis. As a candidate, Thomas followed the daily order of the canons, shared their hours of prayer and work, and perfected his calligraphic skill in copying liturgical and devotional books needed for use at Mount Saint Agnes. Printing with movable type would only be invented by Johannes Gutenberg (ca. 1398–1468) some fifty years later.

On June 10, 1406, which was the Feast of Corpus Christi, Thomas was invested, by his brother, community prior, with the white habit of the Canons Regular of Saint Augustine, the definitive sign of his formal acceptance into the Windesheim Congregation. Then in 1408, he pronounced his religious vows and began his study of theology, which culminated with priestly ordination in 1414. Thomas was then thirty-four years old. He twice served as the community's subprior; he was first elected to this office in 1425 and again in 1448. As subprior, he not only served as assistant to the prior, the community's superior, but also fulfilled the important position of master of novices. It is most likely that it was during his first term as subprior that Thomas wrote the treatises that make up *The Imitation of Christ*.

Except for the few years of his living in a Friesland monastery (1429–1431) and caring (June 1431– November 1432) for his ailing brother, John, then superior of the House of Bethany, near Arnheim, Thomas' entire religious life was spent at Mount

Saint Agnes. On his return to his monastery that November, after his brother's death, he served as community procurator and in 1448, as mentioned, was again elected subprior.

When not fulfilling administrative positions for the community, Thomas was principally involved in copying books or manuscripts. His skill in calligraphy was such that he was chosen to copy the entire Bible for the community's use. This task took him fourteen years to complete (1425–1439); that Bible's five volumes are today preserved in the Darmstadt Library. From Thomas' pen, in addition to the spiritual and ascetical books mentioned earlier, there also came three biographies: namely, those of Masters Geert Groote and Florentius Radewyns and that of Saint Lydwine (1380–1433), a contemporary of his. In writing that of Master Groote, Thomas received his information from those who had known and lived with him, but when it came to writing about Master Radewyns, Thomas wrote about one whom he knew personally. At the time of Thomas' death, he was writing his *Chronicles of the Canons Regular of Mount Saint Agnes*, a history of the monastery from the year of its foundation (1399), which was also the year when Thomas entered as a candidate. This chronicle is one of the chief sources for information concerning him.

Thomas died on July 25, 1471, leaving the chronicle unfinished. An unidentified brother took up the task where Thomas had left off. Before proceeding on his own, however, he saw fit to insert into the text the date of Thomas' death and added: "He wrote that complete copy of the Bible that we use and also many other books for the use of the house and for sale. Likewise he composed diverse little books for the edification of the young, which books were plain and simple in style but mighty in the matter thereof and in their effectual operation. . . . As age grew on him, he was vexed with dropsy in the legs. . . . [He] was buried in the eastern cloister by the side of Bro. Peter Herbort." The brother then continued the chronicle to the year 1477.

At the time of his death, Thomas was ninety-two years old; he had come to the Mount at age twenty, was on probation for eight years, invested for sixty-four years, and a priest for fifty-seven.

In 1560, because that area had fallen under Protestant control, the monks at Mount Saint Agnes gave up the monastery, and in 1581 it was totally destroyed during the subsequent religious unrest in the Netherlands. Some two hundred years after Thomas' burial, when that part of the country was again Catholic, his remains were unearthed, and in 1672 they were duly placed in the church of Saint Joseph in Zwolle. After that church fell into ruins, the remains were transferred in 1892 to the church of Saint Michael, and when this church was replaced by a newer church of Saint Michael, a short distance outside the old town of Zwolle, the remains were moved (1965) there. Finally in 2000, they were given a permanent resting place in Zwolle's magnificent, centrally located Church of Our Lady.

The Treatises

The chapters in both treatises are brief and to the point. *A Little Garden of Roses* comprises eighteen chapters, while *The Valley of Lilies* has thirty-four. One may wonder why Thomas chose these titles for his work? The answer most probably lies in his reading of one of his favorite authors, Saint Bernard of Clairvaux. In Bernard's thirty-second sermon *On the Song of Songs*, he speaks of the beloved "going . . . into the beautiful places of the desert, to the flowering roses and the lilies of the valley, to gardens where delights abound and streams run from the fountains, where storerooms are filled with delightful things and the odors of perfume."[1] By so entitling his treatises, Thomas envisaged the reader slowly strolling through a garden of roses and, on another occasion, walking in a valley blan-

[1] *On the Song of Songs*, trans. Kilian Walsh, vol. 2, Cistercian Fathers Series 7 (Kalamazoo: Cistercian Publications, 1976), p. 142.

keted with lilies. Each of the virtues treated in the various chapters is similar to a rose or lily; by reason of the virtue treated, each is worthy of admiration, and the sublimity of its teaching is similar to the flower's aroma. Just as the stroller in the garden or valley rests in order better to contemplate the flowers before him, so the reader of these treatises is invited to rest and leisurely reflect on each of these virtues.

Both treatises are translated from *Thomae Hemerken à Kempis opera omnia*, edited by Michael Joseph Pohl (Freiburg im Breisgau, 1902–1922) in seven volumes. The Latin text of these treatises will be found in volume 4, pages 1–134. Though Thomas wrote these treatises for his monks, this does not automatically exclude others from reading or profiting from them. All who are baptized, laity as well as monks, are called to praise and love God, do good, and by this means to attain to salvation. What Thomas is preaching in these treatises is valid for all who want to be saved, whether a monk or a layman. When it happens that Thomas specifically refers to life in the monastery, the reader can easily make the necessary adjustment: for example, monastery can become one's home, cell can be one's room, attentiveness during recitation of Office can be attentiveness during one's own prayers, et cetera.

What can be said about the composition of these treatises? Both comfortably fit together, the second being a companion to the first, as the author hints in the preface to the second treatise. As for the date of composition, we have nothing certain; however, it is clear from reading these treatises that they post-date his *Imitation*, for the reader who is acquainted with that earlier text will note its echoes in these works.

Like all meditation books, this one is not to be read at one sitting but prayed chapter after chapter. The author would have you stroll through them slowly, as you would when walking in your rose garden. Pause and reflect on what he has to say, and then join with him when he addresses the Lord and listen to Him when He speaks you.

Finally, the prayer of the translator is that these meditations fill your heart with a greater love for Christ and with a more ardent desire to be united with Him when your days on this earth come to an end.

FEAST OF SAINT JAMES

A Little Garden of Roses

On Seeking Good Companions and Avoiding Those Who Are Evil

With the holy you will be holy,
and with the wicked you will be wicked.

(*Psalm 18:26*)

Beloved brother in Christ, be especially careful not to be seduced by dissolute, corrupt, and evil companions, but associate with a brother who is virtuous, disciplined, and knowledgeable, from whom you will always hear a good and consoling word, worthy of imitation. As a chilled piece of coal grows hot and glowing when placed near a flaming fire, so a lukewarm individual, through association with one who is fervent and devout, also becomes fervent, devout, and enlightened.

In this way the Apostles, through their fellowship with Christ, became holy men, filled with the Holy Spirit. Mark, while accompanying Saint Peter, came to know the holy Gospel, which he heard with great joy from the lips of blessed Peter. In similar fashion, Timothy, working with Saint

In quoting Scripture, Thomas à Kempis uses the Vulgate text.

Paul, became acquainted from the days of his youth with the holy Scriptures. Later, after he had advanced in grace, he was ordained by him Bishop of Ephesus. He was much beloved by Saint Paul as an only son is by a beloved father.

Thus Saint Polycarp, through his contact with John the Apostle, became a powerful and popular preacher of the faith and as renowned a martyr as Saint Ignatius [of Antioch]. Our most blessed Father Augustine,[1] having been instructed and baptized by Bishop Saint Ambrose, later became a glorious Doctor of our holy Church, and his name is now illustrious throughout the world. Thus the holy youth Maurus, joining with Saint Benedict, later became, with God's assistance, a holy Abbot, famous for his virtues and miracles. Bernard, beloved of God, on entering the Cistercian monastery under the venerable Abbot Stephen [Harding], became the light of his religious order—like a brilliant star illuminating the heavens. Many are the examples, ancient and recent, that confirm that good companions bring blessings to the soul, while dealings with the depraved bring it harm.

Good reading is profitable, while unbecoming conversation is harmful. Solitude together with silence is beneficial, while uninhibited worldly gossip is injurious. Spend your time either alone with

---

[1] The religious congregation to which Thomas à Kempis belonged was the Canons Regular of Saint Augustine.

God or with a devout companion, conversing about Christ's virtues. Do not be curious about searching out higher things; apply yourself to knowing your own vices and to making use of the proper remedies for your deficiencies.

2

On Fleeing the World
and the Devil's Snares

A wise man shall hear and shall be the wiser.

(Proverbs 1:5)

Young man, who seek the good, attend to the words of eternal wisdom, which are of greater benefit to you than that of all this world. Hold fast to Saint John's words, "Love not the world or the things that are in the world";[1] rather look upon all things as if they were dung and poison. Give thought to your end without end, and all temptations will cease. Stay clear of all danger to your soul; keep from being a source of scandal to anyone, and refrain from unbecoming speech.

If your father, according to the flesh, attempts to draw you away from God, tell him that you have a Father in heaven. And if your mother or sister tries to oppose you, answer them: "You are but mortals and subject to error. He who has created me will Himself guide me." To the one who serves God, no good thing will be lacking.

---

[1] 1 John 2:15.

Commend all your friends to God, praying that they amend their lives and ever be on guard against sin, lest they, for the sake of earthly things, offend God and lose those of heaven. Too frequent visits of friends brings much disquiet to the heart. "The world passes away and the desire thereof";[2] you, too, will pass away and all your friends with you.

The devil's snares are many, and whoever desires to be rich and to appear powerful succumbs to his myriad temptations. Each day we encounter his snares: in food and drink, in a roving eye, an idle tongue, an inconstant heart, in growing weary doing good works.

All is vanity—honor, wealth, and power. For what are you searching? What do you wish to find in this world, where everything is tainted? All is vanity, fleeting and deceitful, except loving God and always doing good.

You cannot love God perfectly unless you despise yourself and the world for the sake of Him, "who repays a hundredfold in this world and life everlasting in the world to come".[3]

Oh, Brother Pilgrim, may you not find it difficult to distance yourself from those friends and acquaintances who often are a hindrance to eternal

---

[2] 1 John 2:17.
[3] Mark 10:30.

salvation and a cause for the withdrawal of divine consolation.

Where are those companions of yours with whom you laughed and in whose company you delighted? I know not; they have left and deserted me. Where is the enjoyment of yesterday? It has vanished. Where are the meals and the drink you had? They are all gone. Did abstinence do you any harm? Not at all. Therefore, he is accounted as wise who serves God and wholeheartedly spurns the world and its pleasures. Indeed it is so.

Woe to all who have become intoxicated by this world's charms, whom, sooner than not, the upright will avoid, flee, and bury. See, they have all died.

Never again will they return to me, and I, too, will be following them whenever God calls. They were guests on this earth, and so am I. They have left all, and so must I. Suddenly, like a shadow have they passed away, and so will I.

3

On Seeking True Wisdom in God

Blessed is the man who finds wisdom.
(Proverbs 3:13)

Seek the true wisdom that Christ taught and ex-
emplified in his own life. The truly wise man hates
iniquity, speaks the truth, and acts with justice. He
lives a chaste and humble life, and is likewise devoutly pious, sober, and careful in staying clear of
grave temptations. Such a man is indeed wise and
pleasing to God. He enjoys a good reputation and
has a clear conscience; he avoids worries, experiences peace, and God frequently grants him such
joy of heart as the world has never known or enjoyed.

All that the world considers wise is vanity and,
in God's judgment, foolishness. This wisdom deceives those who have become enamored of it, and
it is ultimately the cause of their torment.

The wisdom of the flesh is, indeed, the death
of the soul, for it quickly carries off those fond
of imbibing wine and who indulge in worldly delights. Yielding to the degrading pleasures of the
flesh only results in sorrow and punishment. True

wisdom, however, is drawn from Christ's hidden words and sacred actions, by means of which he urges us to despise the world, flee its delights, conquer our flesh, endure suffering, undergo labors, and love virtue.

4

On Struggling against Our Vices

The kingdom of heaven suffers violence.
(Matthew 11:12)

Many begin, a few continue on, but only a handful arrive at perfection. This is because we either yield too easily to the flesh, pridefully build ourselves up, or collapse in the face of adversity. How rare it is to meet someone who seeks God selflessly, who conquers himself completely and gives himself thoroughly over to God.

A certain devout person once remarked: "Perfection is like a rare bird because to conquer oneself is most difficult." The one who does not strive to attain virtue will never taste its sweetness, for every virtue carries within it its own proper relish, which refreshes him who diligently strives after it.

He who engages in wickedness prepares a ruinous end for himself, for he forfeits his self-respect, extinguishes his peace of soul, meets with sorrow, increases his sadness, and loses all savor for good. On the other hand, he who abstains from pleasures, even those that are licit, grows more secure against those that are illicit.

He who muzzles a dog no longer fears its teeth, and he who observes strict silence does not offend with his tongue. Whoever chooses to be silent and reserved distances himself from lies and calumnies, curses and quarrels, anger and grumbling. It is easier for one to avoid the above and to keep one's mind free of them by not engaging in malicious conversations and in not seeking useless information.

The custody of the senses is the bedrock of purity, as discipline is of peace and one's cell is of devotion. When anger takes hold of a person's thinking, wisdom then departs even from one who is prudent. Whoever speaks in wrath is like a barking dog; but whoever responds with gentleness breaks through the other's wrath and offers him roses rather than thorns. Blessed is the tongue of the prudent man, for it heals the wounds of one in anger. Whoever struggles against his vices at the very outset, when their motions are first felt, will have greater success in overcoming them than if he delayed until they became rooted.

As an experienced gardener carefully plants roses and lilies in his garth, so that he can enjoy them at some future date, so also he who is faithful to his exercises of devotion, to prayer and meditation, which are indeed heavenly things, will one day enjoy the company of angels in the celestial paradise. He who preserves purity of mind and body is similar to an angel, but he who gives way to his vices and finds pleasure in vile thoughts is nothing but the slave of the devil. It is indeed difficult to resist such motions, but future punishment—being tormented in eternal fire—is still more difficult to bear.

Heat is conquered by heat; one nail is driven out by another; and laughter is expelled by sadness. When the love of God enters the heart, all that is fleeting must take its leave.

He is truly wise who can spurn the thousands upon thousands of this world's delights. All things are as nothing, including being a king or a pope. The end of all things is death, worms, and ashes. No matter how highly one may extol himself, he is actually nothing, for death despoils him of everything. Happy is the pilgrim who has a home in heaven.

5

On Acquiring the Grace of Devotion

Woe to you that laugh, for you shall weep.
(Luke 6:25)

Since virtue cannot coexist with vice, it follows that devotion cannot be acquired by means of laughter and banqueting, but in silence and mourning. Perfect virtue is not acquired instantaneously, but only little by little and with much pain and groaning. There must also be a firm purpose of making progress—each day more and more—and of doing violence to oneself by fasting, vigils, prayers, meditations, work, study, writing, abstaining from useless conversation, and the willingness to remain in solitude.

Every joy that does not have God as its author quickly dissipates; it also stains and is harmful.

Edifying speech is pleasant to the ears, while harsh words cause distress in a friend and idle words are a waste of valuable time.

Be diligent in doing good and patient in bearing trials; this way you will find happiness in life as you spend your every hour praising God.

Rarely will you be without one or the other—

sadness or joy. Happy is he who sees good in all things and benefits from adversity.

Whoever loves God receives from Him, with equanimity, the bitter and the sweet, and gives thanks for the same. He stands firmly and safely who places his hope in God and not in himself or in another man.

6

On Hearing and Reading the Divine Word

Blessed are they who hear the word of God.
(Luke 11:28)

Human consolation is useless if it proves an obstacle to divine consolation. When holy Scripture is read, it is God speaking to you; therefore, hear God's word with a grateful and humble heart. Truth is not to be spurned, even when announced by someone simple. Whoever lives an honorable life is a good teacher, and whoever reads well is God's messenger.

The faithful messenger remains silent when it comes to what is harmful, makes known what is salutary, and knows not how to invent. Pure truth is always pleasant to hear.

Esoteric discourse is harmful to the untrained, and that which is full of flattery is dishonest. The one who tells false tales disrupts another's peace, for those who hear them cannot help but be led astray.

The discerning judge is worthy of all praise, but one who is harsh and implacable is not worthy of mercy.

One who yields to anger is his own severe torment; such a one often harasses the innocent, covertly castigates those in authority, and blatantly ridicules those who do good. Whoever speaks deceitfully finds none to believe him and has very few friends.

It is good to be silent when it comes to what is evil; it is holy to make truth known, and desirable to act with modesty. It is just to harm no one, pious to be of assistance to all, and devout to edify the neighbor by word and example.

The prudent man acts after much thought and does not seek anything new without good cause. He does not readily speak of what he is ignorant, nor is he apt to agree to what is doubtful.

A silent tongue is a great help in achieving peace of heart, while the mouth of the fool is almost continually open and ready for argument.

Whoever desires to be pleasing to God will watch over his heart and tongue lest he lose the grace of devotion and offend those who love silence. Many fine words do not fill the bill; nor do eloquent words sanctify those who are idle or ambitious. He who does well will have it well.

On Divine Consolation amid Tribulation

*The Lord is nigh unto those
who are of a broken heart.*

(Psalm 34:18)

No one is so good and devout as not to encounter some worries and troubles in life. When you face tribulation and are sorrowful in heart, you are with Jesus on the Cross. And again, when through the grace of the Holy Spirit you enjoy consolation in prayer, you rise, as it were, with Christ from the dead and the tomb, and with a jubilant heart you celebrate Easter with Jesus in the newness of life.

When someone directs harsh and unkind words against you, you are given to drink of the chalice of the Lord as medicine for your soul. Remain silent and drink of the cup of salvation without complaint, for the Lord will be your protection in life and in death. God will not forget you. There is nothing more admirable than to remain silent and patient, for in this way you curb the mouth of him who utters evil against you, and at the same time you follow the example of Christ, who remained silent before Pilate, though much false testimony had been brought against Him. You are no better than God, who, for your sake, endured scourging, ridicule, and death at the hands of the wicked.

A man does not know how good and virtuous he actually is until harassed by his enemies. Christ has many friends who claim that they love Him and are willing to share a meal with Him, but there are only a few who are willing to abstain with Him.

The true lover of the Crucified, in order to conform himself to Christ hanging on the shame of the Cross, does not flee from suffering, nor is he troubled by the wayward. For him who sees Christ as his life, suffering, and dying for Him are accounted a great reward.

The more fervently one loves God, so much less does he fear death and the greater is his desire to be dissolved in Christ so that he may live happily with Him and eternally enjoy the company of the angels in heaven.

Happy the soul that loves Jesus with tenderness. His love for things eternal permits him to despise transitory goods, and for the name of Jesus he patiently endures evil and prostrates himself at His feet, praying for an increase in virtue and perseverance in his good resolves.

8

On the Joy of a Good
Conscience in the Holy Spirit

Rejoice in the Lord always.

(*Philippians 4:4*)

Rejoice with those who are good, endure the bad, have compassion for the sick, forgive those who do wrong, and pray for everyone.

Cast aside from you all gloom and depression, for these breed indifference and bitterness. Adopt the practice of devoutly meditating on the life and Passion of Christ, and you will find true consolation against all temptation and sadness.

A good life deserves praise, but a lukewarm conversation is a burden to oneself and to others. A good conscience engenders joy, while a bad conscience means torment for oneself. Strive always to do good, and you will be at peace. As long as you walk firmly in the right path of the just, the evil plots of the wicked will not harm you.

A man's good conversation results in joy of heart and earns him a reputation that is praiseworthy. Empty flattery dissipates as soon as it leaves the lips of the one uttering it, and insincere praise spoken by a fool is more harmful than a blunt correction from one who is just.

Humble prayer rises to heaven, pleases God, obtains grace, and drives away the devil's deceits. Humble confession merits forgiveness, while frivolous excuses aggravate the transgression. True contrition wipes away the stain of sin, and fervent amendment of life lessens punishment.

Useless chatter decreases the grace of devotion, but good conversation increases our joy. Careful custody of the senses is everywhere necessary, and the cloister proves helpful to one who wanders about.

Frequent prayer is a firm protection, and a silent tongue makes for a peaceful dwelling. Many begin fervently, but it is perseverance that receives the crown of glory.

Christ's yoke is sweet to those who love, a burden to the lukewarm, bitter to the proud, light to the meek, and dear to the humble. Jesus makes all things sweet and light.

The carnal man always seeks what is light and easy, but the spiritual man hates and flees from such. The just man suffers greatly because he is unable to extinguish all the hateful motions that rise within him. Why does God permit this? So that man may always humble himself and continually implore the divine assistance.

As the proud man rejoices in honors and the rich

man in wealth, so the man who is truly humble rejoices in his self-contempt and in his lack of worldly goods. Christ, King of Heaven, is the glory and wealth of the servants of God.

Outside of God all delight is depraved, all joy is empty, and all abundance poverty. Nothing satisfies the soul's hunger except God alone, who created it. The soul's great freedom resides in not desiring anything of this world.

The life of the just man is to do good and suffer evil, to praise God in all things, and never to yield to pride because of the good he has done.

The man who truly praises God loathes himself, thinks good thoughts, expresses them, carries them out, and then ascribes all this to God.

Do not yield to temptations of vainglory, but frequently and with humble heart say with the prophet: "Not to us, O Lord, not to us; but to Your name give glory."[1]

Man enjoys his greatest triumph when he conquers what delights, overcomes what causes fear, and calmly endures what brings bitter pain.

[1] Psalm 115:1.

9

On the Good Conduct of a Brother Who Is Humble

God gives grace to the humble.

(*James 4:6*)

Every word and action that come from a religious brother ought to be wrapped in humility and modesty and not have anything to do with trivial matters.

A good sign of future virtue in novices and the young is humble conduct and spare speech, especially when with their elders. Whoever does not accustom himself first to listen and to be silent will rarely be numbered among the learned and the wise. Many are judged to be fools because they lack good manners.

Prompt obedience, frequent prayer, devout meditation, diligence at work, eagerness for study, love of solitude, and not being a busybody are what make a monk devout and bring peace to his soul.

In Genesis we read that God looked favorably on the gifts of Abel but rejected those of Cain. Why? Because Abel was innocent and humble, while Cain was jealous and dissolute. Be another

Abel, patient with vexations, and do not pick a quarrel with Cain, otherwise you will forfeit your internal peace and good reputation. It is better for you to lose what is yours than to offend God, injure your brother, and violate charity.

If you wish to gain a heavenly treasure, cast aside the heavy load of this earth. If you crave lasting honor, despise this world's glory. If you desire peace, avoid the places where controversy arises and anger is aroused. If you wish to be great in heaven, be small in the eyes of the world. Do not justify yourself before men, for human praise is of little worth when a bad conscience is the accuser.

The foolhardy individual as well as he who is loquacious are censurable, for neither observes good manners. Many of the strong have fallen because they depended too much on themselves, while many infirm have recovered their health because they hoped in God and invoked His name.

When one is humble and meek, he renders himself lovable to all; but the one who is austere and unbending is avoided by all around him.

The patient and silent man wins over his enemies through kindness and charity. The one who willingly serves others and sympathizes with the troubled finds that his friends grow in number.

Whoever does not know how to remain silent at the proper time embarrasses himself before others.

He is accounted prudent and wise in conduct who knows how to be good and advance in virtue.

Whoever fights strenuously against his vices is reckoned as courageous and resolute, and he who exercises dominion over his evil inclinations is accounted an excellent master.

The soldier who controls his body with the arms of chastity is well protected and invulnerable, and he who lives chastely on earth is worthy of living with the angels in heaven. The chaste man is a friend of God, a companion of the angels, a kinsman of virgins, and a beloved fellow citizen of the saints. Whoever is humble and chaste overcomes demons and instills fear into the shameless.

Outstanding is the superior who conducts his life along the path of the virtues and gives good example to his subjects, and he who strives to imitate these virtues is worthy of a good man's praise. Noble and honorable is the man whom virtue ennobles.

The man who is free of sin is indeed attractive, but the sinner, though he be adorned on the outside, is, nevertheless, black within. He who is filled with God's grace and does not covet honors is both wealthy and happy.

The one who loves what harms him and dismisses what benefits him can be said to be insane and an idiot. It is divine wisdom to seek the everlasting goods and to despise all that is transitory.

If anyone asks you to be his teacher, show him the way of humility and walk before him as an example. The truly humble man does not know what it is to be inflated; rather, he spurns praise, enjoys contempt, and quickly forgets the injuries done him.

10

On the Instability of the Human Heart

He who abides in Me and I in him,
the same bears much fruit.

(*John 15:5*)

The thoughts and affections of mankind are unstable and vary greatly, and those that do not come from God are tainted and worthless. O human heart, full of desires and never satisfied! How bitter and wrong it is for you to abandon your God. Why do you contemplate so many foolish things, all of which are completely incapable of consoling or fully satisfying you?

What will you then do? Where will you turn in order to have it good? Return promptly to your heart, reflect on how many ways you have given offense, and see that you make amends for the evil you have committed. Prepare there a dwelling for God. Keep yourself free from all inrushing thoughts and outside concerns so that you may become filled with the consolations of the Holy Spirit.

Whoever is in the habit of wandering away from

his monastery is rarely made any better. All that glitters in the eyes of the world is as good as nothing. Whatever is seen does not satisfy the one seeing, and whatever is heard does not fill the heart. Unless everything is geared to praising the Creator, then all that you see is useless.

Hence holy David, with lyre in hand, sang these praises to God at every assembly: "By Your deeds, O Lord, You make me glad, and at the works of Your hands I rejoice."[1]

One will not find stability in any created good, but only in God, who is the Supreme Good. Stand firmly in the truth, and the truth will set you free from all deceit, iniquity, and falsehood spoken against you. All that is maliciously fabricated about a neighbor will revert to the head of the fabricator.

Christ is truth, and whoever follows Christ is a lover of truth and of all virtue. Whoever abandons truth for temporal gain or honor loses faith and the beauty that comes from virtue. God is truth and will not permit liars to remain hidden for long. The evil one may be able to disguise himself for a time, but the truthful man will finally prevail, and the one who utters falsehoods will be reduced to confusion when he least suspects.

Do not think of or desire anything other than

[1] Psalm 92:4.

what is right and especially pleasing to God, that is, the virtues and good works done in God's honor.

Remain in truth and charity, and you will be acceptable to God, to the angels, and to men. Be not afraid. The evil one may be able to withdraw some transitory things from us, but God gives to those who are patient things much greater and eternal.

If you desire peace and a good conscience, observe humility, patience, and obedience. When your passions become overly excited, there is no worst enemy than yourself. If you look carefully at your own defects, you will give little thought to those of others.

II

On Having Trust in God in Difficult Times

Hope in God and do good.
(Psalm 37:3)

No one is foolishly to rejoice in temporal goods or place too much trust in friends and relatives, for all things are uncertain and fraught with danger. On the other hand, whoever trusts in the Lord and calls upon Him when in need will not find himself abandoned in time of tribulation.

Great peace is promised the one who lives a good life, speaks of holy things, harms no one, and endeavors to free himself of all wicked and evil thoughts. Close the door of your house, and you will dwell in peace.

Whoever does not plan on performing some good deed each day—this serves as a shield against the devil's attacks—will find that he falls very easily.

When things do not go well, many cease praying and give up fighting temptation. Virtue is only had by labor and much toil, and it is only preserved by exercising much care.

A brother who loves to wander and ignores house customs detests a disciplined life and the quiet of his cell—as a bird does its cage.

If you are seriously tempted or sorely corrected or ridiculed or embarrassed or despised, do not yield to despair, but remember that you justly deserve to be despised and punished because of your wickedness. Bear all with patience, and confidently say: "Lord it is good that you have humbled me, that I may learn your statutes."[1]

It is in time of temptation and trial that an individual, because of his dire need and the gravity of his faults, learns that God is more necessary than ever to him.

He is accounted a foolish and unfaithful servant who, because of his master's wealth, puts on airs and despises all others. Whoever despises his fellow servants and considers himself better offends God and all the saints. This is a great error in us and comes from the fact that we are not humble and do not pay attention to our own defects, which should always be before us and for which we should continually weep.

It is enough for each one to carry his own burden. What advantage is there in meddling in others' affairs and taking on more than we can handle?

Sometimes it happens that a man's weaknesses,

[1] Psalm 119:71.

mistakes, and negligences become publicly known, so that, being embarrassed in the presence of others, he can humble himself the more, learn to have compassion on others' weaknesses, and be of assistance to those who err. From his own experience, he can say: "This is a man and not an angel. It has happened to him as it has happened to me. In this we are brothers. While I knew I was doing wrong, he may have thought he was doing well!" There is only one who never errs or yields under temptation, and that is God alone.

Why laugh at another's fault? "If anyone thinks he stands upright, let him watch lest he fall."[2] Laugh at your own lapses. Public embarrassment is often the best means for bringing vainglory to an end.

[2] 1 Corinthians 10:12.

12

On the Power of Prayer and the Usefulness of Pious Reading

Pray without ceasing.
(*1 Thessalonians 5:17*)

Why pray without ceasing? Because trials and temptations surround us on all sides, as do the snares and enticements set by the bad angels.

Rarely is good news heard today. Warfare is being waged everywhere—there is fear within and conflict without. No day is free of strife, nor is any hour without the horror of death. These battles and conflagrations are the just judgment of God because of men's sins, and by these scourges He urges the elect to set their hearts on what is heavenly.

Ceaseless prayer is, therefore, especially necessary to counteract all the dangers of this world and to serve as a sturdy breastplate against the attacks of the enemy. Whoever does not pray does not fight; and he who does not fight or show resistance is quickly conquered and forfeits the victor's crown.

But who can always pray and continually fight? All things are possible to him who calls upon God and puts his trust in Him. For "God is near to all who invoke him in truth."[1] If you are unable always to pray with your lips, then pray in your soul and in your heart; pray by your righteous desires and good intentions.

The sincere desire always to do good and to serve God is a sacrifice made on the altar of the heart. He prays always who always seeks to do good. Whoever laments his past sins and longs to perform good works in the future prays without ceasing. Say with holy David: "O Lord, all my desire is before You, from You my groaning is not hidden."[2]

The word of God and pious reading are very useful in bringing peaceful calm to the soul when it is distracted by different tasks or burdened down by some sorrow or other. Reading points out the right way to live and offers examples that spur us on to imitation, while prayer asks for the grace enabling us to follow them. Reading about God is good, praying to God is better, but praying for love of God is by far the best. Blessed is he who directs all his words and actions toward praising God. May God be all in all, be blessed above all, and praised forever and ever.

How can one who finds greater delight in telling tales than in reading and prayer be said to be religious, or how can he become devout? Whoever

[1] Psalm 145:18.
[2] Psalm 38:9.

eagerly listens to frivolous tales and passes on trivial matters sells his soul for a paltry sum.

In every trial and temptation, have recourse to prayer—the safe haven of your soul—and implore the divine assistance. The sooner, so much the better; the more you delay, so much the worse. The more often you pray, so much the more helpful, and the more fervent, so much the more acceptable to God. God, who is holy and merciful, wishes to be asked; He provides opportunities for prayer and promises to hear them, for He said: "Ask and it will be given to you."[3]

By His words, God exhorts us to pray; He encourages us by His examples, cautions us by His commands, comforts us with His gifts, punishes us by trials, gives us joy when things prosper. This we meet every day of our lives.

God also grants an experience of internal sweetness to those who pray devoutly, who enjoy solitude and willingly keep silence. This same He denies to those who spend their time roaming about and engage in useless chatter.

Whoever desires to hear good news, let him listen to Christ as He speaks about the kingdom of God, about future judgment, the heavenly Jerusalem, the joy of those dwelling in heaven, and the orders and choirs of angels who rejoice without

[3] Matthew 7:7.

end. Let him hear the prophets as they foretell the mysteries of Christ's life and with thundering voice predict punishment for sinners.

Let him hear the Apostles and the Evangelists as they straightforwardly narrate Christ's teaching and miracles. Let him listen to the Doctors and read their admirable sermons in which they clearly explain obscure scriptural passages, exhort us to adorn our lives with virtue, and refute errors and heresies.

Let each one take from all this what pleases him and what serves his needs, not spurning what is simple or reproving what is noble because it surpasses his understanding. It is pointless to censure the wise and unjust to judge holy saints.

Endeavor humbly first to learn and then to practice the less important matters, and if it be to your benefit, God will then grant you to understand what is more important, for it is written: "When a man knows the right thing to be done and does not do it, then he sins."[4]

A man may know much and may read a great deal, but if he never makes use of what he knows and what he has learned, he walks away empty from a table that is wonderfully spread. He who prays rarely and works sparingly will long remain cold and poor.

---

[4] James 4:17.

Whoever speaks out against vices and does nothing to overcome his own sows good seed among thorns. If anyone approaches prayer without first fortifying his heart against evil thoughts, little fruit will be had, though he speak many a word.

Happy the man who carefully guards himself and casts from him all impurity and does not allow what offends the eyes of God to remain hidden in the depths of his heart.

Humble confession of sin before God cleanses away all vices in a heart that is both humble and contrite.

The devout man finds delight in prayer, the student in books, the pious man in virtue, the proud man in honors, the humble man in contempt, the wealthy man in riches, the miser in money, the beggar in alms, the glutton in food and drink, the idle in frivolous speech, the sober in abstinence, the wise in wisdom, and the good monk in the observance of his rule. It is the love of God and a good conscience, however, that bring about joy and delight.

If you wish to conquer your soul's worst enemies, then take flight and seek silence and quiet. Pray, fast, study, and work. The holy man thinks holy thoughts, speaks the truth, acts properly, and spurns present realities to contemplate those that are eternal. The humble man listens to counsel; the prudent man avoids dangerous occasions; the patient man piously puts up with annoyances; and the diligent man does not neglect his tasks.

Whoever does not avoid small defects will fall into greater ones. He who is lukewarm in the morning rarely becomes fervent by evening.

Whoever casts off sloth and takes up some occupation is blessed with internal joy and merits great honor—if not from men then certainly from God, which is to be desired and preferred more than anything else. For God Himself is the reward of all honest labor, anxiety, and sorrow and is the crown of the saints.

The idle man is not satisfied by trivial talk. The virtuous man even abstains from what is licit. He who is grounded in humility and counts all the honors of the world as nothing is the one who stands upright and walks along the correct path. He thinks wisely and acts sensibly who strives to please God alone, who flees external affairs, seeks what is internal, desires the heavenly, loathes earthly things, despises himself, and always prefers the love of God to all other good things.

13

On the Praise of Charity and Its Fruits

Let all your actions be done in charity.
(1 Corinthians 16:14)

Charity is a noble virtue, superior to all other virtues, knowledge, and gifts. Charity embraces God, unites angels to men, and transforms the sons of men into sons of God and friends of the saints. It was charity that made Christ be born of a virgin and be crucified for our salvation. Charity cleanses the soul from sin and draws it to love God with one's whole heart, mind, and soul; it also inflames it and fills it with a marvelous sweetness.

Charity justifies sinners, makes slaves into free men, enemies into friends, foreigners into fellow citizens, strangers into acquaintances, and wanderers into settlers; the proud become humble, the stubborn meek, the lukewarm fervent, the sad happy, the stingy generous, the worldly heavenly, and the unlearned wise. All this comes about through charity, which is poured into the hearts of the faithful by the Holy Spirit and given them from heaven.

The wings of charity are large and wide, and thus

it flies above the Cherubim and Seraphim and all the choirs of angels. Through charity the many are made into one—uniting those above with those below as well as those in the center; it likewise produces joy in one and all, a joy not derived from vainly glorying in oneself, but a joy that is rooted in divine love.

Charity envelops heaven and earth, land and sea, and all that is seen or heard in creation is directed to the praise and glory of its Creator. There is nothing so small or insignificant in nature's realm that is the goodness of its being; it does not manifest the work of its Maker, the power of its Creator, the wisdom of its Designer, and the providence of its Governor, who rightly rules all things. Such a consideration draws the devout soul to praise God and to bless, acclaim, and exalt Him in every place and at all times.

Because of charity, the soul glows inwardly, just as wax melts when placed near a fire. Charity cannot be restrained, for it ascends high above all the stars of the heavens in search of its sole delight, the Creator of all things and Ruler of all, there to rest securely and find its happiness in Him. Oh how pleasant and delightful it is for him to whom it is given to be near God and to enjoy being with Him. Oh, would that it were permitted to me to experience, even in very small degree, what is clearly accessible to the angels, and this without end.

However, we must return to our active life and through the virtue of charity strenuously struggle against our daily temptations. It often happens that after great consolation there comes profound desolation, or troublesome temptation, or bodily unease, or aggravation on the part of men, or loss of friends, or attacks of the enemy, or disturbance of soul, or derision from children or reproof from elders, or harsh correction by superiors.

All these are designed to humble the pride in our hearts, so that we might have compassion on those who are ill as well as on those tempted and troubled. Therefore, we are not to have confidence in ourselves or to have a taste for things above us or to seek anything that is to our own advantage, but in true charity we, who are subject to God, ought to humble ourselves in all things and before every creature for the love of God.

It was through charity that God came into the world and through charity that He led mankind back to heaven. It was through charity that Christ descended to sinful man and through charity and the shame of the Cross that He ascended to the Father's right hand and gave mankind the greatest of honors.

Charity is never indifferent, for it concerns itself with things that are important and sublime as well as things that are humble and abject. It carefully engages itself in things that are honorable and finds delight in the lowly things that obedience enjoins upon it. It does not pull back from touching a sick man's wounds, from washing his feet, preparing his bed, laundering his clothes, or removing filth. Patiently it bears with things that are arduous and finds joy in the reproaches paid him.

As fire consumes wood, so charity snuffs out vices. It cleanses the heart by contrition, washes it by confession, dries it by prayer, enlightens it by pious reading, inflames it by devout meditation, promotes recollection by solitude, and unites the soul to God by fervent love.

Charity inspires the mouth of man to praise God, his hands to work for Him, his feet to walk in His footsteps, his eyes to contemplate His goodness, his memory to recall His graces, his body to serve Him, and his soul to love Him above all good things both in heaven and on earth.

When charity dwells in a humble soul, it annihilates past failings, strengthens it for future combat, instructs it about things present, delivers it from many doubts, restrains it from being inquisitive, does away with superfluities, rejects vain things, exposes the false, hates what is shameful, softens the hard, casts light on the obscure, discloses the secrets of heaven in prayer, and orders all things within and without.

In a soul that is holy, charity is ready goodwill, which does not cease working, though at times bodily weakness and necessity may keep it from accomplishing the good it originally intended.

Happy is the pure soul to whom God is all; who feels that nothing outside of God is pleasant or precious and views all things as bitter and burdensome. Such is the one whom God seeks and whom God loves, namely, one who for the love of God despises himself and all things, gladly abandons them, fights strenuously, and keeps his heart pure.

Quickly and freely the pure soul continues on toward God, fleeing all the savory things of this world and desiring neither comfort nor honors while on this earth. The charity of Christ liberates us from the world's bonds, makes all heavy burdens light, and grants us enough strength faithfully to fulfill whatever is pleasing to God. Hence he prays with Christ and says with Him: "Father, not My will, but Yours be done always and everywhere."[1]

[1] Matthew 26:39.

14

On Watchfulness and
Combating Temptations

Resist the devil, and he will fly from you.

(James 4:7)

No matter how intimately a good person may be in union with God, that is, by prayer, meditation, study, or writing, the holy angels are there rejoicing with him as are the devils to distract and tempt him. When you begin to pray, the devils flee as from the fire of the Holy Spirit, but when you fall into idle conversation, they all speedily return to urge you on in your frivolous talk. Should a conscientious superior come upon such a gathering, he will immediately disperse the idlers and reproach them for wasting time and neglecting their duties.

Therefore, live your life in silence, and look upon God as your consolation, and as long as you persevere in the way of life you have chosen, the monotony of good works will not disturb you.

Be faithful in little things, and your reward will be ten thousand times greater in the kingdom of heaven. If you keep from being idle when alone or talkative in public, the devil, outmaneuvered, will leave you. He loathes the brother who works and keeps silent, who prays and meditates.

Wherever you may be, alone or with others, you must fight, watch, and pray against the temptations of the flesh and of the spirit. Fight strenuously, pray fervently, study much, cherish silence, and suffer patiently. Always place your trust in the Lord—no matter how severely troubled or desolate you may feel.

He who always and everywhere exercises patience will enjoy greater peace in this world as well as victory over his enemies, and with the elect in the next he will receive a brighter crown of glory.

15

On Bearing One Another's Burdens

Bear one another's burdens.

(Galatians 6:2)

Since we are all one in Christ, we must maintain
fraternal charity, which binds us together in peace,
and work in harmony for the common good. We
are all members of Christ, reborn in baptism by
the grace of the Holy Spirit, redeemed by the Passion of Christ, cleansed by the blood of Christ, and
nourished by the body of Christ. Furthermore, we
are instructed by the words of Christ, confirmed
by the miracles of Christ, and guided by the examples of Christ.

My brothers, why then would you wish to hurt
one another? Whoever injures another, by word
or deed, also offends Christ, who will avenge and
punish the evil done unless the guilty one quickly
amends his ways.

Inasmuch as we have one Father in heaven, God,
we are all brothers of Christ, and it matters not
from which city or country we are gathered here
or whether our parentage be noble or lowly. The
one God created all of us, governs us, and cares for

us; He has called us by His external word, and daily by interior contrition He calls us to the one beatitude, our final end. This one God has promised to give Himself to us as our future reward in the presence of the angels and amid the universal happiness of the citizens of heaven.

Therefore, since we are all called by this one God, redeemed by one price, and imbued by the one Spirit, let us then endeavor to love and serve one another. If we wish to be pleasing to Christ, then let us bear one another's burdens and in charity pray for one another, for God is in each of us, and each of us is in God. Whatever imperfection or foolishness we witness in a brother, we ought to interpret it kindly, as we would wish it done to us.

Beloved Brother, bear with others, and they will bear with you; excuse others, and you, too, will be excused. Have compassion on the sinner, and compassion will be yours. Comfort the mournful, and you will be comforted by one in joy. Raise one who has fallen, and by the help of God you, too, shall be raised up. As you do to another, so it will be done to you, for God is a just and demanding judge.

Do not be surprised or astonished if one who is frail should fall in this world, for angels fell in heaven, and Adam was overcome by a puny apple in paradise. It often happens that a man suffers a severe temptation because of something that is indeed very small or because of a simple annoyance on the part of another. Now God justly permits this to happen so that you realize that if you fail in overcoming trifling temptations, you will not be able to overcome greater ones.

Be kind to a brother suffering temptation, and pray for one who is troubled, just as you would pray for yourself. Your good fortune is my good fortune because I rejoice with you, and your misfortune becomes mine because of my compassion for you. Since we are all frail men, we are bound in charity to pray for one another.

The person who fails to see his own defects ought not to censure another; for him to despise another's faults is like a blind man mocking another blind man or the deaf laughing at another deaf man or a fool ridiculing another fool.

Maintain silence with regard to another if you have no authority to admonish him; rather, look to yourself, and correct what you find there. If you think you are right and still intend to set your neighbor straight, then first begin with yourself and only later proceed to correct him, but with modesty and prudence, setting aside all hostility.

If you sincerely love me as a brother, then treat me as you want to be treated, and pray for me. Whoever corrects another and does not pray for him lacks sympathy; he is not a gentle physician but a cruel enemy and a garrulous talker.

He who prays for another as he does for himself performs two worthy deeds. The more one is imbued with fraternal charity, the more willingly will he pray that the other may amend his life and no longer give offense to those who are weak. If, however, he refuses to listen to you and your admonition, then deeper will your grief be. We are to each other either a fragrant rose or a piercing thorn.

16

On Loving Christ and Despising the World

Remain in my love.

(John 15:9)

The voice of Christ is a voice sweet to our hearing and salutary to all when obeyed. The love of Christ is the joy of the mind and the paradise of the soul; it shuts out the world, conquers the devil, closes hell, and opens heaven. Love of Christ and love of the world are contraries; they have nothing in common, nor can they exist together. The love of Christ is Elijah's chariot ascending into the heavens, while the love of the world is the devil's cart descending into hell.

To love oneself is to do injury to oneself. To forget the world is to discover heaven. The flattering phrases of a false friend are more harmful than the sharp correction of a just man. When a deceitful person sets about thinking, he invents lies, whereas the thinking of a just man proceeds logically unto the truth. Whoever scandalizes another will himself be the victim of scandal.

God, who rules all and knows all things, does not

long allow His little lamb to stray and to continue its bleating, but He either leads it back by the staff of fear that He carries or reclaims it with a loving glance that penetrates its inner being.

Where there are peace and concord, God is there with all His benefits, and where there is strife and dissension, the devil is there with all his snares. Where there is humility, there is wisdom. Where there is pride, there is the root of all evil; conquer pride, and you will find much peace. Where there are harsh words, the soul of charity is wounded.

Where there are silence and solitude, there the monk finds repose. Where discipline and commitment hold sway, there a religious makes spiritual progress. Where laughter and dissipation reign, there devotion flees. The idle and talkative individual rarely feels compunction and is rarely free from sin.

Where there is prompt obedience, there is a happy conscience; where there are lengthy conversations, there work is neglected; where there is self-promotion, there charity is lacking. Where the teaching of Christ flourishes, there the soul advances toward salvation; where there is harmony among brethren, there is unity; where moderation is practiced, there concord perdures. Where discretion is observed in correcting another's faults, there no one can voice a just complaint or have reason to become angry with his superior. Someone once said: "Be moderate in all things, for moderation is a most attractive virtue."

Where there is patience, there one gains a victory over the enemy; where disorder reigns, peace departs quickly. Keep your lips tightly shut, and weigh your words before speaking. Where there are faith and truth, there peace is guaranteed. Where there are deceit and iniquity, there are devious thinking and futile planning. Where there is charity, there is the Holy Spirit. Where there is even slight mistrust, there is frequent resentment; where truth is known, there is joy in the heart. Where falsehoods are spoken, the underlying purpose is often to deceive a friend. Where there is humble confession, forgiveness is easily had. Where worldly wisdom proves insufficient, divine protection is to be more earnestly invoked.

Whoever maliciously excuses unjust actions will himself come to an evil end. There is much peace for the one who does well and exercises himself in patience. Woe to the impious man for his evil deeds and to a deceitful man for his alleged good actions, because their iniquity brings more injury to themselves. Where there is duplicity, there is inconstancy and much wickedness. All goes well with the just and simple man who knows no guile, for God is with him, directing all his actions and keeping him on the right path. As for the man who does not honor his own word, is there anyone who will readily believe him? But if anyone changes his word for something better, he does not thereby violate the truth.

It is a delight to hear about good deeds done, but it is more praiseworthy to perform them. The best self-examination leads to amending one's life, and its fruit is to abstain from sin and to advance in virtue.

The fruit of devout prayer is the union of one's heart with God under the inspiration of the Holy Spirit. He prays devoutly who shuns all vain thoughts. Whoever places the image of the Crucified before him quickly drives out the devil's suggestions. The soul's most beautiful exercise is recalling Christ's Passion. Whoever reflects daily on Christ's sacred wounds soothes, cleanses, and cures his own soul's wounds.

Whoever looks upon all earthly goods as filth and does not long for honors achieves purity of heart and can rest undisturbed in God. He praises and honors God to his utmost ability who profoundly humbles himself and carefully recalls his defects and then grieves and weeps over them.

True contrition of heart, together with a humble acknowledgment on the part of the sinner, is a strong voice in God's ear. Whatever good you do, do it to the praise of God. He who simply and entirely, purely and willingly refers all his virtuous actions and all the good works of others to the praise and honor of God—ascribing everything to God and attributing nothing to his own merits and powers—strips and divests himself of all that he has and at the same time tramples underfoot invidious pride and stamps out vainglory.

He who rejoices in himself and not in God, who alone is our Supreme Good, deprives himself of eternal honor and glory. Thus, the Blessed Virgin Mary exultantly sings in her holy canticle about the exceptional gifts granted her: "My spirit rejoices in God my Savior."[1] And the Apostle Paul writes: "If any man thinks that he amounts to something, when in reality he is nothing, he deceives himself."[2] Though Paul was taken up into the third heaven, he did not boast because of this, but whatever good he had done or taught or wrote, he attributed all to God, saying: "By the grace of God I am what I am."[3]

---

[1] Luke 1:47.
[2] Galatians 6:3.
[3] 1 Corinthians 15:10.

17

On Imitating Our Lord Jesus Christ's Most Holy Life

*As long as you did it for one of these,
my least brethren, you did it to Me.*

(*Matthew 25:40*)

Pay attention to the following, note the mysteries therein, and take them as examples to be imitated.

He who assists a brother in need holds Jesus by the hand. He who patiently bears the burdens placed upon him carries Jesus crucified on his shoulders. He who speaks consoling words to a saddened brother gives Jesus a tender kiss.

He who regrets another's fault and prays for his pardon washes and wipes Jesus' feet. He who remakes an angry person into one of peace prepares a bed of flowers for Jesus in his soul. He who at table places the best portion before his brother rather than himself places before Jesus a feast and a honeycomb of charity.

He who attentively meditates on God welcomes Jesus into his heart's inner chamber. He who offers a book of sacred readings to a brother offers Jesus choice wine. He who keeps from idle conversation drives the flies away from Jesus' table.

He who refuses to listen to slanderous speech and reproves those who speak unbecomingly drives out, with the staff he carries, the vicious dog from Jesus' house. He who reads clearly and distinctly while his brothers dine brings joy to those at Jesus' table and with this heavenly cup inebriates the thirsty. He who reads poorly lessens the savor of the food, and he who reads badly stains the cloth on Jesus' table.

He who hears of another's evil deeds and sorrows and grieves because of them anoints Jesus' sacred wounds. He who speaks of his neighbor's virtues and good deeds places beautiful flowers before Jesus' eyes. He who devoutly reads and proclaims Jesus' words spreads fragrant aromas before his audience.

He who kindly tolerates and finds excuses for another's faults will readily experience Jesus' mercy. He who declines to speak of a neighbor's vices and scandals spreads a garment over Jesus' naked limbs. He who seriously reflects and meditates on Christ's holy miracles and humble deeds receives milk and honey from the mouth of Jesus. In this manner did the blessed Agnes speak and act, who likewise shed her blood for the love of Jesus.

He who sings or reads to a brother who is weak and infirm joyfully plucks the harp before Jesus' crib in union with the angels. He who prays devoutly, abstains from the finer foods, and renounces all his belongings places, together with the wise men, three precious gifts into Jesus' hands. He who washes the heads and clothing of his brothers baptizes Jesus together with Saint John the Baptist.

He who keeps to his cell and observes silence enters the desert with Jesus. He who resists his evil inclinations and chastises his body fasts with Jesus. He who speaks a salutary word to his brother preaches the kingdom of God with Jesus.

He who perseveres in prayer for a brother who is weak and tempted visits Lazarus with Jesus and weeps with Mary and Martha. He who celebrates Masses for the faithful departed and recites the Divine Office for them comes with Jesus to Lazarus' tomb and asks that he mercifully deliver their souls from punishment. He who goes with his brothers to the common dining room to hear sacred reading eats and drinks with Jesus and his disciples.

He who retains in his heart God's word heard while at table reclines with Saint John the Apostle on Jesus' breast at supper. He who humbly and promptly obeys in times of adversity follows Jesus and his disciples to Mount Olivet, where He was betrayed and arrested. He who fervently and urgently prays in time of temptation and tribulation joins Jesus in His agony, struggling against the devil.

He who totally relinquishes both his likes and dislikes fulfills with Jesus the will of His Father and carries his Cross to Calvary. He who prays for his enemies and willingly forgives those who have sinned against him joins Jesus in praying for His enemies that they may not perish but be converted to God and live. He who voluntarily renounces all that belongs to this world and assigns all things seen to oblivion dies with Jesus on the Cross and is taken up with Paul into paradise.

He who keeps his heart pure and peaceful wraps Jesus in a clean shroud and entombs Him in his heart. He who perseveres unto the end in serving Jesus sleeps and pleasantly rests with Jesus in the tomb. He who shares in the Blessed Virgin Mary's sorrows will be comforted in his difficulties by her and her son Jesus.

He who recalls Jesus' every word and deed and relishes them prepares for Him a sweet aromatic ointment well suited to bring comfort to a saddened soul. He who humbly and devoutly offers thanks for benefits received comes with Mary Magdalen carrying sweet-smelling perfumes to Jesus' tomb. He who after contrition and confession of sin firmly proposes to amend his life rises with Jesus from the death of sin.

He who casts off his soul's sluggishness and takes on new fervor celebrates a new Easter with Jesus and in chorus with Him sings a jubilant *Alleluia*.

He who spurns all of this world's joys and flees its dangers by entering the religious life enters with Jesus and His disciples into the reserved banquet hall so that he may serve God with greater freedom, live in greater purity, and receive the Holy Spirit in greater abundance. He who brushes aside all temporal things and whose heart, because of holy meditation, burns only for heavenly things proceeds to ascend with Jesus into heaven.

Blessed is the soul that can say: "To live is Christ and to die with Christ is gain",[1] for he who desires to live for Christ must die to himself, and he who desires to enjoy and relish being with Christ must relinquish all ephemeral things. It takes much effort to relinquish these things, and there is sadness in dying, but eternal salvation is living and reigning happily with Christ.

When will it be that God alone will be my all and I will be only His, entirely united to Him? As long as the faithful soul is not united to God in glory, it cannot be fully happy. Therefore, throughout your life, follow Christ, walking in love and in fervent faith and charity, that face to face you may be worthy to see Him, who grants beatific joy to the angels. May Jesus Christ, who bore the bitter Cross for all of us, deign to lead us after death to that beatific intuition.

---

[1] Philippians 1:21.

18

On the Eternal Praise of God

His praise be ever in my mouth.

(Psalm 34:1)

How sweet the sound of these words in the ears of the devout, but sweeter still when sung in the presence of God and the holy angels. If all musical instruments were to play together and not resound to God's praise, they would play in vain. The music would neither give pleasure nor bring satisfaction to a devout soul. God and His honor must be the reason for this music. If praise is to be pleasing and acceptable to God, then all vanity must be set aside. If the reasons for your song are pure, then you will exult with Mary with a truly joyful heart. The most beautiful harmony, both in heaven and on earth, is praising God with a pure heart, acknowledging His immense goodness and unsurpassed grandeur, and this in union with all creation.

It is a most pleasant duty to praise God at all times, to love the Creator of heaven and earth, and, most of all, to do homage to the Bestower of eternal life. Indeed, the life, homage, and glory of the holy angels is to praise God with all their being, and never are they to cease from that praise. In this they never grow weary, nor do they ever sing their praises in vain.

The souls of the saints in their heavenly home— now free from the bonds of their bodies, the snares of the devil, safe from all his temptations, united to God in perfect charity and endless joy, and filled with unspeakable beatitude—are occupied in the same way. In their freedom, they recall with much happiness the many trials and sorrows they experienced in this unhappy life and how many temptations and dangers they escaped. Their lamentations are now turned into chants of joy, and their afflictions give greater brilliance to their crowns.

Happy that homeland where everything is peaceful, where there is no sadness but only joy, and where all is filled with divine praise and abundant rejoicing. Therefore, faithful soul, bless the Lord of Heaven, and you, Sion, weighed down by the sluggishness of the flesh, praise your God. When undergoing a trial, call upon Jesus to assist you, and may He be at your right and left together with His holy angels.

Pray that the assaults of the devil do not get the upper hand over you and that the weakness of the flesh lead you not astray; let not the rigors of the religious life weaken your spirit or your labors weaken your body. For the love of Christ, take up the burden of the Holy Cross, which will open the gates of the kingdom of heaven for you. What more do you want? The royal road that leads to Christ lies in conquering your own will, bearing with your shortcomings, and not seeking bodily comfort. In exchange for a modicum of labor, you will certainly enjoy eternal happiness and eternal honor for your humble and low rank.

Therefore, let the praise of God be ever on your lips, in good times and in bad, for you can gain much merit from this if you fully resign yourself to God's will. Whatever sorrows afflict you from within or without, accept them humbly and gratefully as coming from the hand of a kind Creator, who cares for us all—both the great and the small. He who made you in His image will not, out of His immense goodness, desert you when you are in need. Therefore, open your mouth in praise of the omnipotent God, by whose providence everything in heaven and on earth, in the sea and in its inner depths, are ruled.

Praise your Creator, who made you a man and not a beast, and if He had made you a fly, He would still be worthy of your praise, for He had made you well. The lion cannot boast because of his strength over that of a fly or a gnat—the lion may roar the louder, but the fly flies the higher.

Therefore, let there be no arguments between the great and the small, between the rich and the poor, between the strong and the weak, between the wise and the simple, between master and servant, but let all equally praise the Lord God, who created all creatures in a vast variety and with marvelous beauty. All these He created for the praise and glory of His holy name and generously and unreservedly placed them under man's command.

Faithful soul, praise your Redeemer, who by His Passion and sacred Cross redeemed you from the grasp of eternal death. Even if you were to be crucified and die a thousand times for Him, you still could not offer Him adequate thanks.

Praise your Protector, who has kept you from countless sins and dangers. Praise your Benefactor, who has granted you so many favors that you can scarcely count them. Even to this very day He bestows new gifts on you, and for your benefit He comes to you on the altar and supplies you with the best gift He has, which is Himself, and this He communicates to you. For these gifts He asks nothing more from you except that you love and praise Him for His sake and with your whole heart.

When you are happy and all things are going well with you, offer praise and give thanks, because the good Lord has deigned to grant you consolation, lest you languish on your way. As often as you read and hear the word of God or meditate on Christ's Incarnation and Passion, that is how often He sends you bread from heaven.

When you are sad and feel weak, offer praise and give thanks, because God is visiting, testing, and purifying you, lest you yield to pride and rely too much on yourself. Bodily affliction is often a means to repentance of heart.

When you are healthy and feel strong, offer praise and give thanks, because God has given you the capacity to work and serve others, and never spend your time in idleness.

When you are in the garden or in the orchard looking at the different plants and trees—apple and pear—hardy bushes, flowering roses and fragrant lilies, offer praise and give thanks, because God is revealing to you His many marvelous works that shoot up from the earth. Through His wonderful power and wisdom, He renews all these year after year, in accordance with His unmatched goodness and for man's advantage.

Therefore, praise and give thanks to God in every place and at all times because the entire earth is filled with His majesty and His glory is above the heavens. In union with all the saints on earth, praise God, whom all the angels praise in heaven. In praising Him, you become like the angels; on the other hand, by not praising Him, you show your ingratitude and are worse than the beasts.

The birds of the air sing, fish swim, dogs bark, sheep bleat, and all such creatures of the earth are impelled to praise God, for it is by their natural inclinations that they reveal the grandeur of their Creator.

In all that you do, keep God ever before your eyes, avoid giving Him offense, and give Him thanks for benefits received. As you finish each and every task, end by expressing your gratitude to God from the depths of your heart.

Thanksgiving and praise to God, now and forever. Let every spirit praise the Lord! Amen.

~

The Valley of Lilies

Preface

*The just man shall blossom like a lily
and shall flourish forever before the Lord.*

(*see Hosea 14:5*)

This little book can be called *The Valley of Lilies* to distinguish it from the preceding one, which is entitled *The Little Garden of Roses*. Inasmuch as the preceding book treats of many virtues as red roses growing in Jesus' little garden, the present one treats of many virtues as white lilies, planted by the Lord Jesus in the valley of humility, where they are watered by the gentle dew of the Holy Spirit. According to Saint Gregory the Great, whosoever cultivates virtues without humility is like one carrying dust with the wind in his face.

It is with these lilies in mind that in the Song of Songs the spouse of Christ—with humble and devout soul and grateful for His visits as well as His gifts—addresses her spouse, the Lord Jesus. With a song on her lips and great joy in her heart, she says: "My beloved is mine, and I am his; he rests among the lilies",[1] and again: "My beloved is radiant and ruddy, he shall find rest on my bosom."[2]

[1] Song of Songs 2:16.
[2] Song of Songs 5:10 and 1:13.

To Him be praise, honor, and glory, forever and ever. Amen.

On the Three States of Human Life

*I am the flower of the field
and the lily of the valleys.*

(*Song of Songs 2:1*)

This is the voice of Christ as He addresses everyone in His Holy Church as well as each and every devout soul. Christ is the wondrous spouse of Holy Church and head of all the faithful; He is the flower of all virtues, the lily of the valleys, and the lover of humility and chastity.

Whoever, therefore, wishes to serve Christ, the heavenly spouse, and to please Him must strive to overcome his vices, gather the lilies of virtue, avoid idleness, study perseveringly, spend time profitably in preparing books,[1] pray frequently, and seek intimate union with God. He should flee this world's hubbub, love solitude, and shun all extraneous affairs that could cause him harm.

The outward exercise of a virtue without its accompanying interior virtue is of little value before God. An urn may be ornately decorated on the

---

[1] One of the chief occupations of the monks at Mount St. Agnes was copying liturgical and devotional works. Printing with movable type was not invented until the mid-fifteenth century.

outside but be empty within. The pious words and holy deeds of a noble-hearted religious, when directed to the praise of God and the benefit of his neighbor, are like the delightful aroma rising upward from a goblet of excellent wine.

Therefore, my Brother, consider your present state in life, which brings you into contact with other men. Strive to please God faithfully and to edify others, both by your deeds and by religious decorum, for whatever good you do will be credited to you and for whatever evil you do you will be held accountable before God.

Whenever you eat or drink, sleep or rest, or move about wherever you wish, you are acting in line with your carnal nature. In this way you are very much like this world's animals that wander about, eat, and drink until their stomachs are full and then feel sated. If anyone were to try to prevent them from feeding, they would attack with their horns and hooves, put on ferocious faces, snap with their teeth, and growl horrendous sounds. Such are carnal men: gluttons and misers, the proud, the wrathful, and the quarrelsome. These follow their passions because they lack God's Spirit.

But when you keep night vigils, pray, read, and sing psalms and hymns in honor of God and His saints, or when you fast and abstain from wrongdoing, assist your neighbor, lament, mourn, and weep over your sins, confessing them and asking for forgiveness, then you perform works of the Holy Spirit. It is then that you are faithful to the rules of the religious life and walk in its spirit. It is then that you are much like the holy angels in heaven, who continually praise and bless God in song and never turn their faces from Him.

On the other hand, when you give in to pride, anger, detraction, murmuring, telling lies, and disquieting others, or when you find joy in another's ill fortune or are saddened at another's prosperity or when you despise your neighbor and always seek your own comfort, then you are a follower of the devil. In view of your ill will and the evil that you do, you are very much like the evil spirits, who follow their passions and corrupt inclinations—as far as they are able and dare to. Because there is no good in them, they find pleasure in iniquity and strive to seduce and subvert others.

The life of the just man is similar to that of the angels, while the life of the carnal man is similar to that of animals and the life of the proud man is similar to that of the devils. Servant of God, be on your guard not to become entangled in the devils' snares, because on the day of judgment they will denounce and discredit you.

2

On Praising God in Poverty

The poor and those in need
will praise Your name, O Lord.

(*Psalm 74:21*)

If, while praying and meditating on God's good gifts, you find yourself spiritually sad, cold, and dry, do not yield to despondency, nor should you cease calling humbly on Jesus. Rather, in your poverty of spirit, offer praise and thanks to God; and in your search for consolation, readily recite this verse: "The poor and those in need will praise Your name, O Lord."

Many a saint and many a devout individual have, at various times, experienced spiritual aridity, and over a long period of time have felt themselves abandoned by God. This was so that, by their feeling of sadness and utter need, they might learn patience and compassion for others and not to rely overmuch on themselves in periods of fervor and consolation. Together with the prophet, recite this verse from the Psalms: "A beggar am I and poor, yet the Lord cares for me."[1] My trust is in the Lord, for

[1] Psalm 40:17.

He is my strength and salvation. It is indeed true that everything that comes from God is good.

When gladness fills your being, do not yield to presumption, and when sadness weighs heavily upon you, do not give into discouragement. Rather, be content with whatever happens, for all this is pleasing in God's sight. Of yourself you have nothing that is good; all is from God.

When the grace of devotion is granted you, the sun shines in the heavens and your soul glows brightly as one exulting in wealth. But if you deceive yourself by overreliance on self and too high an opinion of self, then wretchedness will be yours. When this grace is quietly withdrawn and taken from one who is ungrateful, then he is truly poor and helpless, for he can accomplish very little and finds prayer tedious. But look upon all this as unto your benefit, for God is humbling you and making you poor along with His elect.

He strikes you on your back with the rod that He uses on His children—and this for your hidden excesses and your many daily omissions—so that you may come to despise yourself and never think highly of yourself. Thus does Saint Paul counsel the Romans: "Be not filled with pride, but be fearful."[2] It is of immense benefit to the soul to have contempt for oneself and wholeheartedly ascribe every good thing to God.

[2] Romans 11:20.

3

On the Devout Being Proven in Adversity

Rejoice in the Lord, you just.

(*Psalm 33:1*)

Endless is the joy in heaven, and endless is the lamentation in hell. Both are also found from time to time in this world, but this is to test the good and the bad.

The days of summer are bright and clear, while those of winter are cloudy and dark. The soul that is devout meets with the same. When God's grace is present, the soul is enlightened and comes to know and understand many things previously unknown, and because of the great devotion it experiences, it gives voice to song and rejoices. In time of temptation, however, when the grace of devotion is withdrawn, the soul feels chilled and frosted—the understanding is clouded over, and the mind becomes fearful. This is when patience is needed and when it is most pleasing to God.

It is by living through times of adversity that virtues grow, and it is in practicing patience that our eternal reward increases. Thanks to afflictions, the soul is humbled and purified, pride is overcome, and vainglory annihilated. As long as the soul remains united with the body, it will encounter adversity and prosperity, and this is so that the soul may grow ever more in the love of Christ. Making good use of good and evil demands much effort, but great virtue is the result.

Therefore, my soul, bless the Lord at all times. Sion, sing the praises of your God day and night, and your reward will be great before God in heaven and on earth. May all things be to your advantage, prosperity as well as adversity, the good and the bad, joys and sorrows.

Thus the Apostle Paul says: "To those who love God, all things work together unto good",[1] and nothing shall be wanting to those who fear Him. Blessed are they who follow God's will in all things.

[1] Romans 8:28.

4

On the True Lover of God

*Love the Lord, all you His saints, both
great and small, because He made you both.*

(*see Psalm 31:23*)

The one who truly loves God loves God genuinely,
that is, he loves God and God alone and desires to
be happy solely with Him—not because of any advantage coming to himself or because of any consolation or reward to be enjoyed hereafter, but ex-
clusively and entirely for God's infinite goodness
and transcendent majesty.

This is why the Psalmist exclaims and frequently
repeats the words: "Give thanks to the Lord for
he is good",[1] words especially relished by those
who love God. But the words that follow, "for his
mercy endures forever",[2] carry a greater sweetness
for those who repent and grieve over their wrong-
doings. Lest the frail and weak yield to despair, the
Psalmist repeatedly makes use of the phrase "for
his mercy endures forever".[3]

---

[1] For example, Psalms 136:1, 106:1, 118:1.
[2] Psalm 136:1.
[3] The phrase is found twenty-six times in Psalm 136, as a refrain.

The man who is more pleasing to God is the one who sincerely tries to be humble and is earnest in expressing his love for God. Blessed is he who considers himself the worst of men and who flees from all that displeases God. Blessed is he who fulfills his daily duties with love and pure intention and solely for God's good pleasure; his only thought is to do everything for the honor, praise, and glory of God.

Blessed is he who returns to God all that he has received from Him and holds nothing back for himself.

5

On the Soul's Gratitude for
Every Good Thing

*Magnify the Lord with me, and
let us exalt His name together.*

(Psalm 34:3)

Whoever expresses profound gratitude to God, even for the least benefits received, praises God wondrously, for He, who has granted these benefits, is supremely great. Hence, you ought not to look upon what the Most High has freely and lovingly granted you as something trifling or of little worth.

God neither seeks nor asks anything more of us than that we willingly love Him, avoid all that offends Him, and always and everywhere to give Him thanks. God highly values the man who out of true humility belittles and forgets himself, judges himself unworthy of all gifts and benefits, does not flaunt them when received, and does not seek the praise of others.

Greater, however, is the man who like Job, though afflicted under the weight of many troubles, despised, impoverished, tempted, reviled, forgotten, crushed, and ridiculed, blesses God, gives Him thanks, and remains joyful in heart. He endures all this as well as being abandoned by friends for the love of God and views all this as a great gain and refuses to be overcome by them.

Blessed is he who humbly accepts afflictions from the hand of God as did Job and offers and abandons himself totally to the divine will. Blessed is he who always seeks to follow that will and chooses whatever is more pleasing to God; he who accepts the worst as the best rejoices when he meets with insult and endures temporal afflictions, knowing they are for his soul's benefit.

6

On the Devout Soul's
Conformity to Jesus Crucified

I am with him in tribulation.

(Psalm 91:15)

Lord, what means this statement? Clarify for me the meaning of the words You have spoken, and explain their intent for Your servant's benefit.

Listen, my son. When you suffer tribulation and your heart is filled with sorrow, you are on the Cross with Jesus, and when you find consolation in your devotions and delight in singing hymns and sacred songs, you rise with Jesus in newness of spirit. It is then that with joyful heart you will sing Alleluia, as one raised from the dead and freed from the tomb.

However, when you pray for your sins on bended knee and with great sorrow beg forgiveness, you are knocking earnestly at heaven's gate. And when you set aside all earthly cares and deep within you meditate on heavenly things, then together with Jesus you continue on your way to heaven in order to dwell there with the angels.

Therefore, no matter what happens or how oppressive the situation, be meek, humble, and patient—and this for the love of God. With patience, carry your cross together with Jesus, and die daily on the Cross for your eternal salvation. Every affliction patiently endured in the flesh is medicine for the soul, satisfaction for sins, and hope of future beatitude and glory. Amen.

7

On the Pure Soul's Walking with God

Walk while you have the light.
(*John 12:35*)

He walks with God in the light who desires to possess nothing in this world and who has fixed his heart on God in heaven, for there alone is the soul's hidden treasure, the Lord Jesus Christ, in whom all good things are found.

He who does not have God as a friend is always wretched and in dire want, but he who loves God and obeys His word has God as a friend. This one rightly obeys God's word, never speaks a useless syllable, practices what he preaches, does not seek his own glory, and continually refers all the good that he himself does or sees another do to the praise and glory of God. On the other hand, whoever is pleased with himself pleases a fool and at the same time is displeasing to God. Therefore, in all the good you do and say, strive to be pleasing to God so that you may receive still further blessings from Him.

Why glory in this world's goods when you are mortal and will soon be eaten by worms? Young man, listen to one who is your elder: Withdraw from all worldly distractions, for you will not find rest unless you look into your heart and seek God above all things and love Him intimately.

8

On Peace of Heart and Finding Rest in God

And his place is in peace.
(Psalm 76:2)

Who is the one who possesses true peace? He who is meek and humble of heart.

Why do you wish to know how it goes with others and in what state they are when you yourself are negligent in many things? He who best knows how to humble himself and to suffer for God is the one who is best at peace. To such a one every burden becomes light because he carries God within his heart. Blessed is he who is in union with God through prayer, holy hymns, and pious reading and who does not gossip about the affairs of the world.

Wherever you are or whither you go or flee, your thoughts go along with you. Pious thoughts bring joy to the heart, while evil thoughts cause sadness. Angry thoughts disturb the soul, envious thoughts blind it, and hateful ones kill it.

Devout reading instructs the soul, prayer enkindles it, and good works flow from it. Edifying conversation cleanses the soul, conceited words stain it, idle discussion hampers it, cruel words bring distress, while pious ones cause it to rejoice. Serious speech strengthens faith, right relationships confirm it, and heavenly colloquies raise it to the heights.

Therefore, cleanse your heart of all ill will, and you will enjoy true peace. True peace is found only in God and with one who is virtuous, for whatever good he does he does for the love of God.

Persevere in silence and put up with all the little things for the love of God, and He, in turn, will relieve you of your disquiet and of all your burdens.

A holy life and a good conscience increase one's trust in God, especially in times of adversity and at the moment of death. A bad conscience, on the other hand, is always filled with fear and unrest.

The man who yields to anger quickly passes from one evil to another, and one that is worse, while he who is meek and humble makes a friend of his enemy and finds that God is always favorable toward him who has shown mercy to a sinner.

9

On Recollecting One's Heart in God

He who does not gather with me scatters.
(Matthew 12:30)

Thus says our Lord Jesus Christ. When you find yourself greatly distracted and devoid of devotion due to countless devil-inspired thoughts or because of your own heart's bitter passions or are disturbed by the unpleasantness of others, seek out a quiet place and recollect yourself, reciting the Lord's Prayer and the Angelic Salutation. Kneel down alone before the Holy Cross or a statue of the Blessed Virgin Mary or some saint's revered image—made to the honor of God and in that saint's memory.

Especially ask mercy of Jesus and of Mary, of the angelic host, and of the entire heavenly court, that the grace of divine consolation be again granted you. Then from the Psalms say with holy David: "Lord, all my longing is known to You, and my sighing is not hidden from You."[1] You have been my hope, Lord, ever since my youth; I now turn to You in this time of trial.

[1] Psalm 38:9.

O Lord, teach me always to follow and to fulfill Your will and to set my own aside, for this is what pleases You and is of benefit toward my own soul's salvation. May it never happen, Lord, that I think, desire, or do anything that displeases You or is injurious to another; this is what You have asked of me and of all who serve You.

If I should do anything contrary to Your will, then in Your kindness correct me and in Your anger condemn me not. You are my God, and because I am your poor and weak-willed servant, I am, in all things and at all times, in need of Your grace and mercy.

May Your name be blessed above all, now and forever!

10

On Watchfulness and Prayer
against Temptation

*Watch and pray, that you
enter not into temptation.*

(*Mark 14:38*)

Be it temptation of the flesh or of the spirit, of the devil or of the world! The flesh excites us to concupiscence and the spirit to pride, and the devil incites us to envy and the world to vainglory.

Christ teaches us the very opposite. He counsels us to be humble, chaste, and charitable and to despise the world so that in this way we may merit the kingdom of God and avoid the pains of hell. Therefore, we must be watchful and prayerful at all times and in all places. There is no place totally secure from the wiles of our depraved enemy, for he neither sleeps nor does he desist from tempting us. "He goes about seeking whomever he can disturb and deceive",[1] continually trying to keep us from accomplishing good and from offering up our prayers.

[1] See 1 Peter 5:8.

For this reason, our Lord Jesus Christ, knowing the devil's malice and the benefits had from prayer, as well as knowing the enemy's strength and the weakness of human nature, earnestly admonishes His disciples and His faithful ones to watch and pray lest they be overcome by their enemies, that is, their vices.

Watch and pray, therefore, that you neither be tempted by the devil nor consent to him. If you are unable to recite the entire Psalter, then read a psalm or a verse or some sacred hymn honoring Jesus, Mary, or one of the saints. By saying these prayers aloud and with some sighing of heart, you will succeed in raising your soul on high.

God is near to all who call upon Him with humility. "The humble prayer of the just man pierces the skies."[2] Such prayer increases one's faith in God and at the same time is victorious over the devil's tactics—his menacing snares and stratagems.

If you are prevented from praying while in the company of others, then follow Christ's counsel and "go to your room, shut the door, and pray to your Father in secret."[3] He is already aware of your thoughts, desires, and needs. Each and every time you pray, pray in this fashion: "Father, may Your will be always done and not mine; do with me as

[2] Sirach 35:17.
[3] Matthew 6:6.

You will, and do whatever is for the good of my soul."

If you happen to be in choir with your fellow monks, sing and pray in unison with them, as do the angels in God's presence. Sing in such a manner that you interiorly experience what your voice externally expresses. In this way you will please your brethren and at the same time not be displeasing to God and His holy angels. God pays more attention to the sentiments of the heart than to the loudness of the voice; He finds pleasure in a prayer that is humble and is offended by every show of vanity.

It is by tears of the heart that grace is received and virtue is increased, but the singing of someone showing off dampens all devotion. For every such fault and failure, an account will have to be rendered.

May the divine mercy protect us from all such evils and lead us to the heavenly kingdom. Amen.

11

On Fear of Eternal Punishment as a Remedy against the Vices of the Flesh

Pierce my flesh with your fear.

(*Psalm 119:120*)

Such a prayer can be helpful against the vices of the flesh and useful in deflating our spirit's pride. These two evils assail us men every day and annoy us because the flesh desires things that are not licit or our spirit, having grown haughty because of some good done, yearns for praise. Both are great evils, and grave dangers can come from both.

When your wretched body—soon to die—is a source of temptation to you, think of the torments of hell's everlasting fire. In this way you will extinguish the fires of concupiscence by hellfire—the stronger motive canceling out the weaker one. It can then be said that the soul is saved "as by fire".[1] All carnal pleasure is of short duration, and all of this world's joys, for example, bodily beauty, honors, and glory, are a deception and a delusion. Just as a fierce headache causes one who is dissolute to

---

[1] 1 Corinthians 3:15.

moan and groan, so the fear of death and the flames of hell can cause one, tempted and about to yield, to abstain from sin.

The man without such fear rushes headlong into sin, and the man who does not humble himself before God and His saints will, on the day of judgment, find himself overwhelmingly shamed by the demons and severely tormented by them. True, certain, and irrevocable remains the statement, applicable to men and angels: "God resists the proud and grants His peace to the humble."[2] The Lord's mercy toward His saints and elect is from eternity unto eternity.

Therefore, you who are proud, fear God's judgment in all that you do, and do not glory in the flimsy reputation that is yours. When you have done all that you could and ought, much still remains, for you have only accomplished one-thousandth. Fear God's rod, staff, and future judgment, for no evil deed will go unpunished and no good deed will go unrewarded.

If your room were on fire, would you not, in your terror, speedily get up and rush out? The thought, horror, and fear of future endless punishment should do the same to you. Having a great fear of hell dispels all lukewarmness and urges us on to fervent prayer.

[2] James 4:6.

12

On Remembering Our Lord's Passion
as a Remedy against Dissipation

*Blessed are those who mourn,
for they shall be comforted.*

(*Matthew 5:4*)

Who will comfort them? Surely, it will be Christ who will do so in the secret depths of their heart and not this world with its worthless vanities.

Frivolous speech, shallow words, and frequent laughter are not in keeping with Christ's sacred Passion and His most bitter wounds. If one sharp thorn from Jesus' crown were to pierce your head or your back, would you laugh? Not at all! As for me, I would sob and cry aloud because of the intense pain. If one nail from His Cross were to pierce your foot, whither could you go or run? I certainly would not be able to move or dash about; I would have to stay put and suffer it. By living with my pain, I would learn to suffer with Christ, and the bitter tears I would shed would be unto the remission of all my sins. Oh, how sacred the sorrow and how sweet the tears when they flow abundantly out of compassion for the sacred wounds of our Lord Jesus Christ!

Therefore, when you feel depressed, tempted, or weak, quickly arm yourself with the shield of prayer and the standard of the Holy Cross; take refuge in Christ's sacred wounds, and, by your earnest prayers and pious remembrance of His Passion, seek the saving remedy for your vices.

Reflect on the weight, breadth, and height of that Holy Cross on which the naked Jesus Christ hung, nailed to it by dreadful nails for your benefit. Carefully count the sharp thorns in our Lord's crown that dug so deeply into the Son of God's sacred head and caused copious blood to flow. If you keep these and the other instruments of Jesus Christ's Passion in mind, they will serve as your night-and-day protection, lest the devil, that invidious enemy, discover that your mind is void of all holy thoughts and defile it by insinuating those that are carnal and ignoble.

In remembrance of our Lord Jesus Christ's holy birth, let your bed not be a bed of feathers. His crib was cramped and poorly appointed, but it was filled with holiness. The Child Jesus lay in it, wrapped in swaddling clothes and covered with a bit of straw —He had no silk comforter—and for nourishment He had nothing but His Virgin Mother's milk.

Let the hardness of your pillow bring to mind the chilling hardness of the tomb of our Lord Jesus Christ, who was crucified for you, who truly died, was buried in the depths of the earth, and sealed in with a large stone.

Seek your rest, then, in the peace of Christ. Forget all that is in this world, and look upon everything that this world judges to be great and pleasing as something vile and worthless. You may thus rise with Him in grace and virtue and on the last day be numbered among the elect in everlasting glory. Amen.

13

On Calling upon the Holy Name
of Jesus and That of the Blessed
Virgin Mary, His Mother

Lord, my God, lead my way in Your sight.
(Psalm 5:8)

Your ways, Lord Jesus Christ, are wondrous ways, clear and safe ways, direct and perfect for walking in them. They are likewise peaceful and holy, for they lead the faithful and the humble of heart to your heavenly kingdom.

Wherever you go or walk, or whether you stop and rest, call upon Jesus and Mary, His holy Mother, and recite this sacred verse frequently so that it may guide you on your way: "Lord, my God, lead my way in Your sight." Add this prayer as well: "Dear Jesus, see that I always walk along Your pathways, that my footsteps never go astray in search of anything worthless or that I speak idle words harmful to my soul."

Then take the following words of comfort with you, as food for your journey; hold them firmly as a staff in hand, and pray them often and with great sincerity: "Jesus and Mary, accompany me as

I am on my way; everywhere and at all times be my guardians lest I stray and become lost, and keep my mind free from all dissipating thoughts arising from within and without."

This holy prayer to Jesus and Mary does not take long to recite and is easy to remember. It brings pleasing thoughts to mind, serves as a loyal companion on the way as well as your constant protector. It refreshes the spirit, acts as a loving friend, and is ever ready to help you. It also knows how to direct every poor pilgrim and all who despise the world on the right path leading to eternal life.

This holy prayer is addressed to companions and assistants who are greater and more powerful than those had by any king or prince in this world. They are also the greatest of saints, even above those in heaven and on earth.

When this holy prayer is said fervently, it calls down the protection of the entire heavenly court, which, in all reverence, follows its Lord Jesus Christ and Holy Mary, His Blessed Mother, who is worthy of all praise and of being honored by all. Whoever has these as companions in this life will also find them to be powerful protectors at the hour of death. If you wish always to live and be happy with Jesus and Mary, then never separate yourself from Jesus.

He who carries Jesus and Mary in his heart walks safely and securely. He frequently speaks their names, blesses them with his lips, and applauds them with joyful hands and dancing feet. He praises them with his voice and rejoices having them with him; his eyes yield tears of happiness, and his very being sighs with love; he devoutly kisses them, embraces them in his arms, and reverences them on bended knee.

Blessed is he who sincerely calls upon Jesus and Mary, who greets them devoutly, affectionately keeps them in mind, and greatly honors them; who cheerfully exalts them and wondrously glorifies them; who loves them ardently, speaks of them admiringly, and joyfully sings and acclaims them. Oh, how lovable is Jesus and how sweet Holy Mary, His beloved Mother!

Blessed is the pilgrim who, during his exile on earth—no matter the place or time—is ever mindful of his heavenly homeland, where, in union with all the angels and saints, Jesus and Mary rejoice amid the greatest of happiness and in everlasting glory. Blessed is the pilgrim who does not seek a lasting home in this world but yearns to be dissolved and to be with Christ in heaven.

Blessed is the poor beggar who daily goes about seeking the bread of heaven and does not cease his humble quest until he receives a crumb from God's table. Blessed is he who is called to the banquet of the Lamb and partakes of the Holy Sacrament until he arrives at the heavenly banquet. As often as an individual receives Holy Communion devoutly—or a priest reverently and fittingly celebrates Mass in God's honor—that is how often he spiritually eats and drinks together with Jesus and His Blessed Mother.

Such an individual is a disciple of Jesus and an attendant of the Blessed Virgin Mary, a companion of the angels, fellow citizen with the Apostles, minister of God, relative of the saints, and a friend of heaven. He flees crowds, avoids gossip, reflects on Jesus' words, and carefully guards his heart and his senses lest he give offense to Jesus, Mary, or the saints. He receives blessings and mercy from the Lord Jesus, his Savior, and as soon as he calls upon Him—no matter the place or in what danger he finds himself—his prayer is heard in heaven.

When the disciples were in the boat and feared that they were about to go under, they called upon Jesus, who immediately appeared to them and said: "Why are you afraid? Have faith. It is I, do not be afraid."[1] Jesus' voice is the gentle voice of consolation; at the same time it has the power to protect, the charm to produce joy in others, the goodness to grant forgiveness, and the graciousness to lead to eternal life. Amen.

[1] John 6:20.

14

On Steadfast Struggling against Vices after the Example of the Saints

Be strong, let your heart take courage.

(*Psalm 31:24*)

Just as we learn from the Passion and Cross of Jesus and from the sufferings of the holy martyrs to endure life's adversities, so it is from the Blessed Virgin Mary and the chaste virgins and holy virtuous widows that we learn to overcome the vices of our flesh, to despise riches, flee honors, and seek and love what is heavenly by disdaining all that is worldly.

O Servant of God, strive to imitate the indomitable patience of courage-filled men by resisting the devil and his solicitations and to follow the loyal constancy of frail and youthful virgins in spurning and casting far from you the delights of the flesh and all other pleasures.

If God in His goodness has given you, in your poverty, some temporal goods, do not therefore, wretch that you are, extol yourself, nor should you play the fool by fixing your heart on those goods, for you do not know how long you will be around to enjoy them. Do not desire a long life but a good one, for a good conscience is worth more than all the treasures of this world. The more you have of this world's goods, the more exacting will your judgment be.

How deceptive is the favor and how short-lived is the glory of this world! How delusory it is to seek one's full enjoyment in riches, honors, dignities, and the pleasures of this life, after which there will be, along with the devils, great sorrow, weeping, and endless burning. From these punishments there is no redemption.

On the other hand, how great is the joy of the elect always rejoicing with the angels. The supreme happiness of the good is to be with God and His saints, and this without end. How happy are the men and how wise the virgins who have left all for Christ and by the narrow way have striven to arrive at the eternal homeland!

Know, therefore, all you faithful and devout servants of Jesus Christ, that it is your duty to battle against a variety of temptations—carnal and spiritual—and to be vigilant as well as to pray, fast, and labor as long as you have breath in you. You must chastise your body lest it rise up and lust against the spirit and, by deceiving and prevailing over the soul, pull it down to hell.

What advantage is there in meticulously nourishing the body on earth and later to be severely

tormented in hell? What good is there in enjoying
the praise and honor of men in this life when in the
next we will be humiliated and condemned along
with the impious and the wicked? To be esteemed
a famous and learned man of the world and not
to be counted among the elect in the next? This
will surely be for you a source of much shame and
disgrace as you stand before God and His saints.
However, to suffer for Christ and to be ridiculed
and insulted by the wicked is the highest honor,
praise, and glory, and this too before God and His
saints.

These are the words of comfort that Jesus himself directed to his disciples and to all who suffer
injury and abuse for his name: "Blessed will you be
when men hate you and insult you for My name;
rejoice and exult, for your reward will be great in
heaven."[1] Amen.

[1] Matthew 5:11–12.

15

On Monastic Stability

Be always steadfast in the work of the Lord.
(*1 Corinthians 15:58*)

Tell me, good Brother, are you any better or holier because of running here and there or listening to gossip and visiting many places when you find at the same time that you are keeping yourself from attaining the kingdom of heaven? Blessed is he who, returning to his senses, promptly seeks pardon amid sighs and groans and keeps his mind and body from all such wandering. Woe to you who gad about so often, wasting valuable time and scandalizing others!

There is much peace for him who willingly remains in his monastery, spends his time quietly with God, prays often, busies himself transcribing books, reads the Scriptures with attention, and gives himself to holy meditation. On the other hand, deserving of a severe reprimand is the one who is both lazy and a gossiper. Such a one should not be permitted to be in communication with others, lest, by chance, he contaminate the weak and the simple and by his inane remarks and unbecoming behavior shock and offend the others.

You slothful jokester, fear the future torments of that purifying fire, for there you will suffer the demons' heavy blows for your every idle word and evil thought. It is much better for you to be on your guard, to weep, and to do penance now than later, along with the wicked, to be endlessly whipped and tortured. There certainly is neither laughter nor merriment in a continually burning hell from whence you in no way can be set free.

If one were to give frequent thought to this matter and ponder it seriously, he would quickly come to despise the things of this world and to disdain all that delights the flesh, so that after death he could avoid eternal punishment and attain to the joys of heaven.

But woe now, and more so in the future, to those who give little heed to the divine commands and look lightly upon them as being of no moment because they have not yet known or experienced such bodily punishment.

16

On Divine Comfort after Suffering Tribulation for the Sake of Christ

In the world you shall have distress;
but have confidence, I have overcome the world.

(*John 16:33*)

There is a proverb, quoted by many, saying: "A companion in sorrow is a comfort." Who is this companion, so good and loyal, who knows how to sympathize with the wretched and sick? He is our Lord Jesus Christ, who suffered and was crucified for us and who, in the Gospel, calls Himself the Physician and Shepherd of souls, the Comforter of the afflicted and of the poor, of the infirm, the fallen away, and the wounded. He said: "The healthy have no need of a physician, but those who are sick."[1]

In like manner, holy David, in speaking comfort to those in sorrow, refers to this same companion, saying: "The Lord is nigh unto them of a broken heart."[2] And again in another psalm, addressing all who are tested and tempted lest they yield to

[1] Mark 2:17.
[2] Psalm 34:18.

despair, God Himself says: "I am with him in tribulation: I will deliver him, and I will glorify him."[3]

It is truly a great consolation for those saddened and variously afflicted to know that for our benefit Christ also was tempted, saddened, and afflicted in many ways. If it were not useful and salutary to our souls to suffer and meet with distress in this life, God, who is supremely good and just in all His ways, would not have permitted it to happen.

Who are you to dare to speak out against His stripes, when He spared not His own Son from the scourging, and you guilty of so many sins? Indeed, it is just that an unworthy and unprofitable servant, smitten at most only slightly, not contradict his Master, when His beloved and wholly innocent Son was covered with so many wounds. It is also only just that one who is sick and seeking health drink but a drop from the cup from which the healthy Physician drinks the fullness of bitterness, in order to purge out all death's poison in man and to restore him—mortally wounded in body and soul—and liberate him from eternal death.

In view of the heavier burden placed on his innocent Lord, that of the servant is altogether light. And when the one who is sick gives serious thought to the fact that illness, lovingly endured, means the cleansing from sin and hope of eternal life, he finds that his pain is greatly diminished.

---

[3] Psalm 91:15.

It would be a most unusual honor if a poor servant were clothed in the garments of his Lord, dressed in the purple of the King's Son, and, thus, made fit to attend the nuptials of the eternal King. Jesus' garments are humility of heart, poverty in necessities, patience in adversity, and perseverance in virtue.

Whoever accepts the Lord's chastisements as gifts finds his soul's salvation in them and a more glorious crown awaiting him in heaven. Blessed is he who understands and appreciates the poor and needy Jesus; though the richest of all, He stripped Himself naked for our sakes. Blessed too is he who, for the sake of his soul's salvation, follows Jesus, patiently carrying his cross amid all his daily labors, even unto death.

17

On Guarding the Heart at All Times and in All Places

My soul is always in my hands.
(*Psalm 119:109*)

Nothing is more helpful or advantageous to one desiring to attain eternal life than keeping the soul's salvation always in mind. No matter what books you read or peruse, the soul's only salvation is in God and a good life. Thus the Lord and Redeemer of souls says to His disciples: "What will it profit a man if he gains the whole world and suffers the loss of his soul?"[1]

Whoever frequently reflects on this point and is more duly concerned about his soul's salvation than about temporal gain and feeding his body is like a wise merchant, for he seeks and prefers spiritual and eternal things over those that are perishable. He is one of Christ's good and faithful servants, who turns two talents into four and five into ten and does not hide the one in the earth, nor does he bury it, nor does he scorn it and throw it away;

[1] Matthew 16:26.

rather, he gives it to some poor man that he may pray for him, or he places it on the altar thanking God for even the least gift received from Him.

Blessed is the servant who is faithful and prudent in little things, who puts all his time to good use and does not busy himself in matters that do not concern him. As one made deaf and mute for God's sake, he quietly makes his way through the hubbub of this world, always carrying his soul in his hands before him.

Therefore, do not be curious, making inquiries about the doings of others—unless compassion for your brother and the love of God demand it. Do not hanker after other men's praises, for these are meaningless, and do not fear others' rebukes, for these are harmless. These latter, however, help humble and purify our soul and crown it in heaven. Only the one who knows how to suffer insults and reproaches for the sake of God is worthy of God's high praise.

$\sim$

As You, Lord God, suffered for me, so I ought also to suffer for You and to follow You as best I can. You said to Saint Peter: "Follow me."[2] Ah, Lord, there is so little that I can suffer for You! Often do I plan, but hardly do I do one out of ten. Many are

[2] John 21:19.

my words, but few my deeds! All is my fault; I have no excuse! My sins are on the increase because of my idleness and negligence. What else can I think or say about this, except that I pray and beg Your pardon? Lord, I have sinned; have mercy on me! This is what all the saints before me have done and taught as well as all who are faithful today. Oh, all you saints and friends of God, pray for me, for I am weak, and because I am in great need of help I humbly ask this of all of you.

The Prayer of One Who Is Poor

O my Lord God, holiest of all saints, incline Your ear to the prayer of Your poor servant. Help me and I shall be saved, and always will I meditate on Your goodness and righteousness. Would that I be numbered among the least of Your flock in Your kingdom, which You prepared for the humble and those who love you! I will love You, Lord, my strength, and this with all my heart, as You have commanded me by Your sacred word. You are my hope and my salvation, my only desire. Give me clarity of understanding against all error; a clean heart against all impurity; a solid faith against all nagging doubt; a steadfast hope against all timidity; a fervent charity against all negligence and indifference; great patience against all anxiety; holy meditation against unseemly imaginings; unceasing prayer against the devil's temptations; attentiveness in reading against frequent distractions; useful occupation against boredom and drowsiness; and a holy recollection of Your sacred Passion against my evil inclinations. Grant me, O my God, these blessings, and confirm me in all Your holy words. Amen.

18

On Silence and Solitude

Behold, I have gone far off, flying away;
I remained in solitude.

(Psalm 54:7)

Why far off? Because of the many benefits proceeding therefrom and to keep the heart from being distracted by seeing and hearing too many things. What the eye does not see and the ear does not hear can neither disturb nor bring disquiet to the heart. Therefore, seeking silence and solitude is good for peace of soul and devout prayer. A secluded spot helps achieve this, as does a quiet place far from the hustle and bustle of the world. As a fish out of water soon dies, so also a monk outside his monastic cell soon yields to distractions and is easily tainted.

As soon as the wise bee gathers honey from a flower, it flies away and happily returns to its hidden hive and carefully deposits the honey, so that she can have nourishment through the coming winter. At the same time she seals in its sweet odor, lest she lose the fruit of her labor as she again sets out in search for more. The more securely aromatic fragrances are sealed in a vial, the stronger their fragrance, but once opened and exposed, the strength of the fragrance quickly dissipates.

The more the blooms of flowers are touched by hand, the more quickly do they become bruised, but when protected by a surrounding hedge or wall, they last much longer. Roses growing in an enclosed garden thrive securely, but in public byways they wither and are trampled underfoot. In similar fashion, the restless and inconstant monk, often seen on the road, brings harm to himself, but the monk who avoids crowds and remains at home gains a reputation for being holy. A burning candle is quickly extinguished by the wind but remains aflame when sheltered in a lantern. Thus the fervor of devotion is better preserved in the secret chamber of one's room and is the more easily lost through involvement in extraneous affairs. Therefore, if you wish to remain devout and have peace within you, love silence and your cell.

The one who has outside business dealings with others must be spiritually strong and well fortified so as not to suffer interior harm. For your spiritual advancement, willingly choose solitude and prefer to remain in your cell, as the Blessed Virgin Mary remained alone in her closed room, speaking to the holy angel sent by God to her from heaven. In like manner, a holy angel, a heavenly messenger and faithful guardian of your soul, may visit you and force the evil spirit, with all his phantasms, to withdraw far from you.

A certain devout lover of silence said: "Rarely do I speak at some length with men without some harm coming to my conscience." Another said: "To prefer a conversation to silence, it has to be most edifying." A third remarked: "Noble is the word when spoken in season." And a fourth added: "He who keeps his mouth tightly closed neither lies nor offends."

How pleasant and worthy of praise are the words of a speaker in which there is nothing deceitful, false, vain, or evil. Many speak much but not without peril, for the tongue is prone to evil. Great peace is had by the one who guards his mouth, remains in his cell, and prays often.

Praise the man who is silent and virtuous, chide the garrulous rover, be wary of the fraudulent, avoid raucous crowds, prefer peace and quiet, follow the humble and devout, and, for the sake of Christ who was crucified for you, patiently bear with the one who vexes you.

One of the brothers once asked an older brother: "What does our order's rule set down in regard to our making progress in achieving devotion and interior peace?" This was his insightful response: "Observe the silence enjoined by our founders, avoid idleness and the gatherings of men."

The three things most necessary in any religious order, and which also please God and the angels, are these: laboring manually to overcome laziness, reading and studying with attention to fight boredom of heart, and perseverance in prayer to triumph over the devil's wiles. The holy Fathers, both ancient and recent, have all praised these points.

The brother who is silent and occupied with God receives blessings from heaven and is the one more likely to contemplate the divine mysteries and be enlightened from on high. On the other hand, the garrulous rover, idly roaming about, renders himself unworthy of heavenly gifts and at the same time is bothersome to one and all.

The proud man cannot remain silent for long because he wants to appear learned and to receive the praise of others, and he who speaks presumptuously is the object of everyone's derision. But he who in his modesty remains silent is esteemed by all.

He who has a low opinion of himself and always thinks more highly of others enjoys a high degree of humility, while he who thinks highly of himself and insists on his own opinion, even when contrary to that of God and his community, is unabashedly proud. Pride is the worst of diseases; it is most hateful to God and that which He often strikes down by sudden death. The one who is simple and innocent, humble and obedient, is at all times secure and joyful.

His is a enviable reputation who makes use of few words, eschews trifling matters, speaks of what is worthwhile, and does everything with propriety. Be moderate in all that you do, for of all virtues moderation is the most beautiful. Christ says the same: "Have salt in you, and have peace among you";[1] and the Apostle Paul: "Let your speech be always in grace seasoned with salt."[2] And holy Job: "Can anything unsavory be eaten that is not seasoned with salt?"[3]

The man who is modest and chaste guards his heart, mouth, and all his senses—prone as these are toward evil—so as not to sin and offend God and his neighbor. The one who willingly listens to worthless gossip and passes it on to others knows no remorse of conscience, and it is by not guarding the doors of his heart and mouth that he loses that grace. The monk given to much talking quickly exceeds the limits of moderate speech.

If you had the Crucified Jesus fixed in your heart, then no idle or useless word would slip through your lips. But because you do not have Jesus firmly enclosed in your heart, you often look for outside consolation, which is both feeble and frivolous and

[1] Mark 9:49.
[2] Colossians 4:6.
[3] Job 6:6.

of little help for the sorrows that inwardly oppress your heart. Only Jesus can offer the soul true solace and heal it from all the diseases brought on by our vices. In the matter of a moment and by a single word, He can free the sufferer from all his afflictions, for God's grace is greater in the good than is the guilt in one who is evil.

Why do you listen to the world's empty rumors, which often disturb you and cause distraction of heart? Why do you neglect the sweet words of Christ, capable of consoling you night and day and of bringing you comfort in all your tribulations?

19

On the Refuge of the Poor

To You is the poor man left,
You will be a helper to the orphan.

(*Psalm 10:14*)

Blessed is the poor man who has God as helper in all his tribulation, consoler in his suffering, sole hope and refuge in his final hours, and crown of glory in the kingdom of eternal beatitude.

Poverty is a precious virtue when willingly embraced for the sake of Christ; its eternal reward is residing with the angels in heaven, where thief does not come to steal, or robber to loot, or bandit to kill. By renouncing all that is of this world, the servant of Christ frees himself of the myriad dangers and daily worries that occupy this world's rich. Great is that faithful soul's liberty who, for the kingdom of heaven and the love of Jesus Christ, is without this world's possessions but possesses all things in Christ, who became poor and sorrowful for our sakes, hanging naked on the Cross and having no place to lay His head, not being able to move hand or foot.

Who is there like unto Jesus, utterly poor in every way? Truly, there is no one. This is why His name, and His alone, has been exalted above all things in heaven and on earth and is blessed above all for all ages. O blessed poverty, unless God had first embraced you, your privations would be unwelcome to all. O happy poverty that wipes away the prideful look in our eyes and lessens sins brought on by our many vices.

He is truly poor in spirit who takes no pride in his words or deeds and seeks not a higher station in life, lest he fall the more swiftly. Oh, how wonderful a virtue is poverty, for when the soul renounces all possessions, the gate of heaven is opened to it, the crown of glory is enhanced, and a trouble-filled life lived in the service of Christ merits, together with the martyrs, the palm of patience.

Blessed is he who makes a virtue out of his needs and his frailties, aware that in all that he suffers he is following the will of God. Therefore, you who are poor, do not be overly sad when you suffer want or offended when you are forsaken by your friends and others laugh at you. Turn your heart to Christ, who was made poor and infirm for your sake.

If you always wish to be happy, seek your consolation in God and in God alone. All consolations coming from the outside are nothing, and no matter how splendid they may appear, they are of short duration and bring no satisfaction. So choose Jesus Christ, the Son of God, as your special friend and kin, and for His sake forget all others. Avoid all acquaintances whose intent is to keep you from serving Christ in a holy manner and who try to lure you to the world and to the gates of hell. Jesus Christ tells us: "Wide is the road that leads to hell, and many are they who enter upon it."[1]

Christ alone suffices for perfect consolation, for He gives the kingdom of heaven to all who relinquish the kingdom of this world and its glory. "For the world passes away and the desire thereof",[2] as does smoke in the wind and as the flower withers in the field.

Therefore, Brother, as you continue to serve God, stand most firmly in your good resolve to observe poverty and persevere in your many labors, both night and day, along with your brothers in the monastery, where earlier you had chosen to serve Him. Willingly you have left parents and relatives, and you have given yourself entirely to God, so that with them and all the saints you may enjoy the kingdom of heaven. For a little labor and slight pain in this world, eternal rest in heaven is being granted you.

[1] Matthew 7:13.
[2] 1 John 2:17.

Ponder the wounds of Christ seriously as well as the painful sores of poor Lazarus, and may this benefit you when you are in your agony, near death, and about to leave this world.

20

On the Poor and Sick Lazarus

I am poor and sorrowful, God help me.
(*Psalm 69:29*)

This is the voice of one who is poor and infirm, sighing to God and longing for His kingdom. O you who are poor and infirm, endure the pains of the body with patience as well as the want of food and clothing; this is only for a short time, for you have not long to be here and suffer. Be thankful to God, for it is easier to bear chastisement now with the poor and weak than to be tormented afterward with the rich and powerful.

Recall your past evil deeds, many a time offending God and your neighbor, and suffer the Lord's rod for the remission of your sins, for which same you have not fully repented or made adequate satisfaction. And for your consolation, remember Christ's many frightful sufferings and sacred wounds; it was for you that He underwent a much greater number and more serious afflictions.

Take comfort in thinking of poor and sore-covered Lazarus, who after death was joyfully taken into Abraham's bosom, and rightly fear the fate of the fastidious rich man, who, after many banquetings, was buried in hell, whence he can never be set free. Think now which should you choose for yourself: to suffer for a time and be in want with poor Lazarus and rejoice everlastingly with Christ, or for a short time to delight in the delicacies of that healthy rich man and suddenly die, be buried in hell, and perpetually burn with the devils? To one who is wise, a few words suffice.

Blessed is he who understands and promptly turns from his evil way of life, lest he be damned with the wicked and suffer dire punishment. The one whom the sacred words do not bring to repentance and amendment of life will afterward have, unadvantageously, to undergo severe torment, which will never end. From such suffering, the poor and infirm Lazarus, taken by the holy angels to Abraham's bosom, is free.

Listen to the many benefits that God has mercifully granted to poor Lazarus. I do not think he had rich friends visiting him or servants or companions to wait on him, but as Jesus says: "The dogs came and licked his sores."[1] In his great misery, these alone remained his consolers. What could be more lamentable than that a man should be bereft of all human comfort and be left to the consolation of animals? From the mouth of the poor man, however,

[1] Luke 16:21.

there never came forth an impatient word or complaint, only thanksgiving and words of praise. But to him, to whom human hardness of heart denied comfort, a feral brute showed gentle solicitude.

Therefore, you who are ill, do not complain if you are left disconsolate for an hour or so and feel uneasy because of the unpleasantness of your sickness, but realize that this has come about through the dispensation of divine mercy, and though seriously wounded and burning here, you will not perish hereafter.

Lazarus may have offended God in small matters, but you have offended Him in matters more serious and more frequently. Therefore, bear the inconveniences of your illness with patience, and rejoice in the fact that you are now and then abandoned by men and that with Lazarus you merit to enter the gates of the heavenly kingdom.

21

On the Clear Understanding
of Holy Scripture

*The explanation of Your words enlightens
and gives understanding to little ones.*

(*Psalm 119:130*)

Whatever is written in the Old and New Testaments was written for the instruction of our souls, that we may faithfully serve God, hating evil and clinging to the supremely good God with pure, whole, and perfect hearts, here and hereafter.

Make a humble inquiry into that of which you are ignorant, and that which you do not fully understand respectfully ask your teachers to explain to you, for when God's words are explained, the hearts of little ones are enlightened. If still unable to understand what is obscure, then remain with the simple things along with the little ones, as the Lord Jesus says: "Suffer little children to come to Me, for of such is the kingdom of heaven."[1] Do not rashly set out to investigate what is beyond your understanding, but leave all this to the Holy

[1] Matthew 19:14.

Spirit, and firmly believe them to be true because the Holy Spirit, the teacher of all truth, cannot give witness to anything false.

That many individuals have many doubts is not the fault of or a flaw in Holy Scripture but is due to the blindness of their minds and their negligence in studying the holy books, which have within them the documents necessary for eternal salvation. With great willingness, therefore, read the canonical Scriptures, and give full attention to the commentaries of the learned and strive to understand them. But do not stop praying or celebrating Mass in the name of diligent study, for many a time it is during prayer or Mass that that which is concealed is made clear to the devout, while remaining hidden to those who are merely curious and inquisitive.

It is most helpful for matters to be presented to the little ones and unlearned in simple terms, otherwise what is subtle can be harmful to them. There are times, however, when subtle matters that are well explained can be of help.

Those who pay diligent attention to the reading in choir and refectory and carefully search out the meaning behind the words of the text feed on a honeycomb when they hear God's every word. As long as man lives in a mortal body, he can always learn more and advance in understanding higher things, but he will not attain to the clarity of understanding possessed by the angels or the vision of the blessed until he arrives at the glory of eternal beatitude—and this only with the help of Christ.

Solid and hardy food is harmful to little ones and the sick, but soft food and light drink offer nourishment to infants. Simplified instruments and restrained singing are more pleasing and sound better to those who are ill than loud shouting, which, like harsh thunder, does not charm but causes distress. Frequent flashes of lightning blind the eyes, while light in a lantern sharpens vision. Incautious swimmers drown in deep rivers, but those who more securely cross over on a bridge avoid the water's hazards.

It often happens that a lamb safely makes its way on a level path, where a strong ox falls, is seized, bound, and slaughtered. Thus the one who simply believes and is humbly obedient finds grace, while the one who is self-confident loses what he has. Delving into lofty matters easily puffs up the proud and brings confusion to those seeking self-glory.

I have seen the simple cry out of devotion during prayer, while those who sing and shout with a loud voice feel no such thing in their hearts. Why does this happen? Because the simple and humble man strives to please God in all that he does and says. The voice of the simple of heart is with God in heaven, while the voice of the wandering heart and showy singer is with the people in the streets and city squares.

Whoever pays serious attention to the meaning of the Psalms and reads and sings them with modulated voice tastes the wonderful sweetness of devotion. God is truly gentle and loving to those of upright heart, who seek His glory and not their own praise. Blessed is the word on the lips of speaker and singer capable of moving the listeners' hearts to devotion.

As the cock, before it crows, first rouses itself by flapping its wings, so the good Brother and worthy preacher ought first to amend himself before reproving another, and the good and wise teacher begins with correcting in himself what he notices and reprehends in another.

Thus Saint Paul, in his preaching, humbly calls himself a sinner greater than all others: "Jesus Christ came into this world to save sinners, and I am the foremost",[2] and "I am not worthy to be called an apostle."[3] Why, O blessed Paul, do you say this? "Because I persecuted the church of God."[4] Then, how have you become holy, the vessel of election, and truly worthy of being highly honored? This is not my doing or that of men but is due to the call and revelation of Jesus Christ,

[2] 1 Timothy 1:15.
[3] 1 Corinthians 15:10.
[4] 1 Corinthians 15:9.

from whom I learned to be meek and humble and to follow His Gospel. I attribute no good to myself, but whatever I did or taught I ascribe totally to Him, who by His grace called me to the faith I preach and serve until death. "It is by the grace of God that I am what I am, and His grace toward me was not in vain",[5] but it abides in me and will abide in me until I attain to Him, who redeemed and saved me with His precious blood.

[5] 1 Corinthians 15:10.

22

On the Great Merit Had from Suffering Patiently for Christ

In your patience you will possess your souls.

(*Luke 21:19*)

When anyone speaks harshly to you or rebukes you unjustly, do not yield to immediate anger or answer sharply; rather, remain silent or speak gently, and bear it patiently as Jesus did. When many bore false witness against Him, He spoke not, and when He underwent His scourging, He uttered no complaint. However, if there be need to speak out and it be of help, then answer modestly and calmly as Christ quietly and meekly did when the high priest's servant rudely struck His cheek. In this way you will greatly edify others, and you will free yourself from any embarrassment.

Be patient on each and every occasion, and, when wicked tongues speak out against you, keep a holy silence in answer to their remarks. In every instance be mindful of your soul's spiritual advancement and of the great merit there is in the virtue of patience, which adorns your soul together with the other virtues and leads to your gaining the palm with the martyrs.

Christ taught this and gave us an example in His Passion. When the high priests and the elders of the people accused Him, He said nothing. He made known in deed what He said in word: "Learn from Me, for I am meek and humble of heart, and you will find rest for your souls."[1] True rest and lasting peace are not found anywhere but in God alone, in true humility and calm patience, whereby all adversity is overcome. Therefore, let all your hope be in God and not in any creature—great or small —because without God all is worthless, but with God all is good.

[1] Matthew 11:29.

23

On the Good Conversation
of the Humble Monk

Flee, my beloved, flee.

(Song of Songs 8:14)

Why flee? Because of the world's many dangers, which one engaged in secular matters often encounters.

Whoever wants to be totally taken up with God longs to be alone, to pray, study, and write, and by such worthy employment he keeps himself from yielding to vice and spends his time profitably and in edifying others. However, to him who freely walks about outside the monastery, looking for idle conversation, rarely does it happen that his heart is not tainted and that he does not return less devout to his peaceful and congenial cell.

Holy and modest speech is appreciated by all, while harsh and unbecoming speech is offensive even to friends. He who is truthful speaks the truth, and the one who deceives another by his lies is despised by all. The truly humble man does not seek praise for his good deeds but ascribes all good to God and all evil to himself. He who uses his mouth for lies casts Christ out of his heart, and he who seeks to know things beyond him confuses himself and is justly deceived thereby. But he who speaks plainly and rightly is loved and esteemed by all.

We are all brothers created by the one God, and we are all born sinners through our parents, but by the grace of God we have been called to faith, and through baptism we have been cleansed and made one in Christ. Therefore, no one is to show contempt for another or ridicule or injure another in any way; rather, for God's sake, let each help and instruct the other as best he can, as he himself would wish done to him if he were in need.

Therefore he who by holy conversation comforts one weak in faith extends the bread of heaven to the fainthearted. He who consoles one who is sad offers the cup of life to the thirsty. He who by kind words calms one who is angry daubs the dog's tongue with honey, keeping it from biting someone and causing injury. He who silences one with a loose tongue promotes peace among the devout brothers. He who prefers himself to others shows himself worthy of being put to shame, and he who humbles himself in all things deserves still greater grace and glory. It is by prayer that he who is pious and humble breaks and escapes the devil's snares, which the proud, by their yielding to vainglory, fall into and perish. From these may the good Jesus always preserve us and lead us to the joys of heaven.

24

On Prudent Speech and
Fraternal Compassion

Physician, heal yourself.
(*Luke 4:23*)

Keep this saying always in mind before speaking
and correcting anyone, lest you sin the greater by
unjustly and unkindly censuring him. The mouth
of the just and wise man speaks when it is oppor-
tune and what is fitting, taking into account the
person to whom he speaks as well as his tempera-
ment, lest he offend or repel him whom he wishes
to heal. The mouth of one who is wise and discreet
is similar to a well-adorned golden vessel filled with
ointment, fragrant with balsam, and deserving of
high praise.

It is by your kind words and religious behavior that men of the world are edified: the lazy are
aroused, the negligent admonished, the ignorant instructed, and the devout inflamed. Men are more
likely to despise the world and amend their lives by
witnessing real-life examples than by any barrage
of words flowing forth from this world's wisdom.

It takes no great art or skill to instruct and correct others; but to regulate one's life well, to accept correction humbly, and to be serious about amending one's life is great wisdom in the eyes of God and man.

Learn to place a good interpretation on what is doubtful, and do not judge matters unknown to you; beware of what is clearly evil, refrain from giving scandal, and bear with the faults and manners of those who are weak, and what you are unable to amend commit to God.

Keep in mind in how many ways God has borne with you and bears with you even to this very day, and you still do not change your ways, though you plan and say you will. God, in His mercy, puts up with you, waiting for you to repent, to come to a better knowledge of your faults, to ask pardon with humility, and to keep from looking down on anyone or judging rashly. Therefore, bear with your brother in a few matters as God has borne with you in many.

The devout and humble man makes use of few words, lest by speaking overmuch he disrupts his interior recollection. The proud man speaks with conceit and the angry individual is bothersome to all, and when the latter is so advised he becomes wrathful. The meek man accepts correction without complaint, obeys rather than rebukes, shows compassion to the sinner, and by his actions shows himself friendly to all.

Whoever desires to be set over others demeans himself and exposes himself to many a danger. The one who seeks vainglory does not long remain silent, because he does not wish to appear ignorant; such a one is ashamed to carry out servile or menial tasks or to stand behind others in line or to take the lowest place. The greatest honor, however, is to show humility in all things, to consider oneself inferior to all others, and to wish to be the servant of all for the sake of Christ, who says: "I am in the midst of you as one who serves."[1]

Young man, before you speak, learn first to be silent; in this way you will not embarrass yourself before your elders. It is safer to be silent than to speak like a fool. It is a great art to know how to be silent when admonished and a sign of great wisdom, when in the presence of the wise and learned, to speak at the right and proper time and with modesty and humility. Because the fool does not know the proper time or the manner or the order in speaking, he earns much contempt and disdain for himself and is rightly ignored.

The young man who is brazen and quick to speak is like a fool ready for a fall, but if he listens when instructed, is silent and obedient when corrected, then there is hope for his growth in virtue and he will surely flourish like a lily.

[1] Luke 22:27.

It is unbounded pride to insist on one's own will when it is contrary to that of God and to be unwilling to listen to the advice and guidance of the elders. Because it is difficult for man to keep moderation in all that he says and does and to have constant guard over himself, monks choose silence and seek a quiet place, and, thus, they flee the crowds and spend their time in prayer with God.

25

On the Uncertainty of the Hour of Death and the Quick End to This Life

*Watch, therefore, for you know
not the day or the hour.*

(*Matthew 25:13*)

Fortunate is the soul that often reflects on its final hour, when all things in this life will come to an end—joys and sorrows, honors, and affronts. Happy that simple soul who, for God's sake, becomes a pilgrim here, despising all of this world's pageantry, however great and wonderful.

At that final hour, all castles, villas, and towns will vanish, as also all golden and silver tableware, all fancy foods and spiced wines. The harp, trumpet, pipe, and zither will no longer be heard, and there will be no more mirth or merrymaking, laughter or dancing, shouting or singing. Revelry, too, will be gone from the streets and homes because the hearts of all the living will be reduced to nothing, and all earth will stand in dread before the face of God.

Wise, indeed, is the one who daily ponders these realities and with tears prepares for the future enjoyment of blessings and eternal joys. Blessed is he who, on his own, forgoes the bodily delights offered by this world, where all things are full of traps and snares.

Blessed is the pilgrim who often mourns and weeps in this place of exile, desiring to be dissolved and to be with Christ in the heavenly kingdom. Blessed is he who hates this world and all in it that can lead to sin and like Elijah flees to a desert monastery in order to avoid the many perils that can draw one, if unguarded, down to hell.

Blessed is he who night and day guards against temptation and prays with Elijah, saying, "It is enough for me, Lord, take my soul",[1] for it is better for me to die in firm hope and depart in grace than to see evil done and live amid so many dangers. As long as the soul is in the body and the body is nourished by earthly food, man is not free from sin or exempt from temptation or immune from future falls. Therefore, he is mightily mistaken and deceived who, like one of foolish heart, wishes for a long life and plans on doing much, not knowing whether he will see a tomorrow.

You, who are of noble family and dwell amid riches, think of what you will become after you die and are buried in the earth! What good will all your wealth be to you then? Today a king lives and

[1] I Kings 19:4.

reigns; tomorrow he is nowhere to be found nor is he heard of. Today he sits on his lofty throne clothed in robes of gold; tomorrow, buried beneath the earth and seen no longer. Today, honored by all; tomorrow, remembered by none. Today, universally praised; tomorrow, stripped of wealth, honors, castles, and residences. Today, the handsomest of men and greatest of kings; tomorrow, food of worms and stench to nostrils. As he came into this world naked, so he goes to his grave as any poor man or exile. All of this world's delights and pageantry come to a quick end; grief and pain, sorrow and death come to one and all.

The king dies, the pope dies, and so does the cardinal; they have their successors, but these, too, will die. Indeed, no one is certain of living even one entire day. There is no asking the pope for a bull for not dying or acquiring a benefice that lasts forever. It often happens that soon after receiving a preference or a prelacy, death intervenes and all is suddenly taken away. And so he leaves Rome alone and poor, as he first came.

In our histories we read about many of our ancient fathers who lived a long time that they were this or that and that they did this or that, but the story ends with "and then he died." "We all die, and like waters that return no more, we fall down into the earth"[2] whence we came.

---

[2] 2 Samuel 14:14.

What is our entire life span: nothing but a brief moment in time—like a passing wind, the morning glow that fades, or a guest never to return. As lightning in the sky vanishes in the twinkling of an eye, so do all this world's kingdoms and seasons.

Count all the days, hours, months, and years of your life, and tell me where are they now? They passed on as did the sun's shadow and disappeared as the spider working its web in a hard, blowing wind. There is nothing stable or lasting on this earth, from which Adam and his children were made. Whatever appears to the world to be wonderful, beautiful, and fascinating is worthless and unimportant; therefore, let nothing alluring deceive you or cause you injury. No matter how things may be decorated with paint or ornamented in gold, silver, or with precious gems, they become dull and tarnished when dead and buried. In whatever you do, in whatever place you are, and wherever you go or travel, be ever mindful of your life's end, for you do not know when the final hour will come.

Happy the one who desires to be dissolved with Paul and to be with Christ, for this is much better than living long in the body and being a pilgrim long away from God, violently tossed and pummeled by this world's waves. If you always have Jesus in mind and truly love and daily pray to Him, then you will indeed have hope in the kingdom of

Him who said: "Where I am, there also shall my servant be."[3]

Blessed is that servant who at his last hour will hear this encouraging word of Christ: "Well done, good and faithful servant, because you have been faithful over a few things, enter into the joy of your Lord."[4]

[3] John 12:26.
[4] Matthew 25:21.

26

On the Eternal Praise of God and the Desire for Eternal Glory

Praise the Lord, my soul.

(*Psalm 146:1*)

Praise the Lord, my soul, from whom all good things come and who lives now and forever; it is to Him that you are to refer all things as the beginning and end of all that is good. It is with much gratitude that you are to offer Him heartfelt praise, so that His gifts of heavenly grace may again and more abundantly come upon you until you arrive at the source of eternal life, the land of everlasting light, and the glorious vision of the divine presence.

Indeed, there is nothing better for you, nothing more salutary or sweeter or more joyful or more worthy or higher or happier or more perfect or more blessed than loving God most ardently and praising Him most sincerely. This I say a hundred times, and I repeat it a thousand times more. There is no duty more commendable, no occupation more worthwhile than to love and praise God, your Creator and Redeemer, and this with your whole heart, with your whole mind, and with all your strength. Do this as long as you breathe, move, and think. Do this in word and deed, day and night, morning, noon, and evening, every hour and every moment. Always hold fast to God, completely and entirely, as much as you are physically and mentally able, so that God may be all in all to you, that He may be always and eternally loved, blessed, praised by you, highly exalted above all and before all, and that you may be united to Him forever.

Therefore, faithful soul, exult in the Lord your God as the Blessed Virgin Mary exulted in Jesus, her Savior. Exult and praise your God, who made and redeemed you and to whom you are indebted for His many wonderful benefits and the daily gifts that He so graciously bestows on you and for which you can never give fitting or adequate thanks. Not even if you were one of the holy angels! So give praise and thanks as a mortal man in need of God's mercy and as one always seeking and begging it.

Though you may often fall, sin, and offend God, do not stop praying or praising Him; nor are you to yield to despair; rather, you are to humble yourself and pray. Love, and you will be loved in return, for love cleanses, heals, and makes up for all past failings. Love enlightens and inflames; it drives away sadness and creates joy of heart—such as the world does not know or flesh and blood ever experienced.

Praise God, and you will be praised; bless Him,

and you will be blessed; sanctify His name, and you will be made holy; magnify Him, and you will be made great; glorify Him, and He will glorify you both in body and soul.

But when will this come about, Lord? When will You place perpetual praise on my lips? When will my heart and soul exult with Your saints in glory?

Hold on for a bit longer, and you will see great wonders when the last trumpet sounds. It is then that I shall give My saints rest and eternal life in exchange for all their pains and labors. What more do you want?

Nothing more; You are sufficient for me, my God and Savior; You give eternal life to those who love and praise You. In place of insignificant deeds, You give what is all important; for what is valueless, You give what is most valuable; and for what is perishable, You give something eternal.

Give yourself to God—all that you have, all that you do, all that you know, and all your talents, and you will be dearer to Him than ever before and richer, too. Say with Saint Paul "having nothing for ourselves, yet possessing all things"[1] in God. Though poor, base, and despicable to this world, nevertheless, rich and "always rejoicing"[2] in the Lord, assured that "there is laid up for me a crown"[3] in heaven.

---

[1] 2 Corinthians 6:10.

[2] 1 Thessalonians 5:16.

[3] 2 Timothy 4:8.

~

O Lord God, my salvation and my God, when will the radiant light of Your countenance gladden my heart in Your kingdom? Oh, when will You clear away all my mind's darkness by the light of Your eternal splendor? Oh, when will You, true peace, supreme beatitude and perfect joy, remove from the depths of my being the obstacles that keep me from You? Oh, when, Lord, shall I freely and firmly follow You wherever You lead, without anything contrary hindering me? Oh, when shall I see You clearly and with my own eyes, not in a mirror and or in allegories or figures, in puzzling riddles or parables, in problem questions or scholarly disputes? Oh, when shall I know all that I now believe in from the Holy Scriptures or from my reading of many authors and my hearing, with my own ears, the many readers in different places concerning God, the angels and angelic choirs, the glory and blessedness of the heavenly homeland, or about the peace and indescribable joy of those in heaven? When shall I be there? When shall I come and appear before You and contemplate your Joyful countenance and the glory of Your kingdom with the Seraphim, Cherubim, and all the saints? That hour, however, has not yet come; the gate of heaven is still closed to me. Thus, as long as I am here, I grieve in heart and my lips will lament until I come to You, my God.

27

On Praising the Holy Angels in Heaven

In the sight of the angels, I will sing to You.
(Psalm 138:1)

O King most high, O God most highly to be praised, Creator of all things, of angels and men; how long shall I remain on this earth and be separated from You and from Your holy angels in heaven? How poor and unfortunate am I! How long shall I live among men and eat the earthly bread of labor and grief and be deprived of the bread of angels "having in it the sweetness of every taste"?[1]

O Lord, when shall I hear the sounds of Your praise coming from the mouths of Your angels in heaven, as blessed John the Apostle—living in exile—heard the voice of innumerable angels singing in unison: "Holy, Holy, Holy"?[2] Would that I were one of them and had a voice like unto theirs! How willingly I would sing Your praises with them, chanting heaven's most beautiful hymns and glorifying Your holy name forever. O Cherubim and Seraphim, how sweetly, how beautifully, how

[1] Wisdom 16:20.
[2] Revelation 4:8.

fervently and wonderfully you ceaselessly sing and rejoice before God—never tiring or growing weary in your joy.

To me every human voice I hear sounds hoarse, every song dissonant, every chant lifeless, every piece of music heavy, every harp and instrument out of tune, all the earth's mirth a dirge, all games a time for mourning, all food and drink insipid, all meat fodder, all wine gall and vinegar, all honey poison, all pleasantries grating, all loveliness displeasing, all that is ornate trash, all honor and glory smoke and vanity, all that is noble and precious base and contemptible. In fact, all things are nothing when compared to eternal life, eternal glory, and eternal joy in the presence of God and the angels, who, night and day, sing their highest and ceaseless praise to the glorious Holy Trinity.

Inasmuch as I am unable to ascend to the heights of such heavenly songs or, in my insufficiency, fully understand them, I regret my inability, and humbling myself I kneel before God and men and ask pardon. All my works, Lord, are truly nothing without Your grace and mercy, which You so generously shower on all creatures, and this without number or measure.

"Oh, the depth of the riches of the wisdom and knowledge of God";[3] how deep and everlastingly

---

[3] Romans 11:33.

true Your judgments on the good and the bad, the grateful and ungrateful, the pious and impious, so much so that there is no one who can fathom Your works or justly complain when anything happens unexpectedly. Therefore, my God, be You forever blessed!

28

A Prayer of a Devout Lover of God

*Let my prayer, Lord, be directed
as incense in Your sight.*

(Psalm 141:2)

My Lord God, it is my desire, in union with all Your saints and creatures, devoutly to praise, bless, and glorify You at all times and in all places and always to love You with a pure heart. Because You are my God and I am Your poor servant, I forever desire to magnify and exalt Your holy name above all Your works.

You, my God, are my light and my hope, my strength and my patience, my praise and my glory. You, my God, are my wisdom and prudence, my beauty and sweetness! My God, You are my music and harp, my timbrel and organ, my psalm and hymn, my song and jubilation! My God, You are my helmet and breastplate, my bow and sword! You, my God, are my treasure and capital, my gold and silver, payment for all my debts!

You, my God, are my home, fortress, and palace, my shield and banner! My God, You are my fortified tower and my life's defense! My God, You are my garden and orchard, my greenhouse and cool retreat! You, my God, are my dining hall and table, my food and drink! All food not prepared or cooked by You is tasteless. My God, You are my cinnamon and sweet balsam, my spikenard, choice myrrh, and precious ointment! You are my rose and lily, my wreath and garland. My God, You are my couch and bed, my blanket and covering. My God, You are my light and lamp, my candelabra and constellation! My God, You are my book, interiorly and exteriorly written, my Bible in which is all of Holy Scripture! My God, You are my teacher, instructor, and adviser, my physician and pharmacist.

Thanks to Your mercy and generosity, I find and have all things in You, and whatever I may seek and desire that is not You I recognize as being of no benefit and of little worth. Open my heart to Your holy law, and "restore to me the joy of Your salvation";[1] expand my heart that I may follow in Your way; confirm me in Your words, for there is no other who can help, nor is there anyone, other than You, who can lead me to eternal life. Hear me, my God, when I cry to You—in affliction, in joy, or in health. I commend myself to You at all times, and I bless You forever. Amen.

[1] Psalm 51:12.

29

On Union of Heart with God

*O my soul, turn to your rest,
for the Lord has been bountiful to you.*

(*Psalm 116:7*)

He, indeed, is your rest and your peace, your life, salvation, and beatitude; therefore always refer all that you do, see, and hear to praising God, so that a good and peaceful conscience may be yours. Do not trust, rely on, or rejoice in yourself or in any-one else; rather, depend totally, firmly, and entirely on God and on Him alone, for He is the giver of all good things who works all in all through His immense goodness and bountiful mercy.

Who will grant me this grace to refer all things to the praise and honor of the Lord, my God, that I may rightly do what I need to do and am able to? Let nothing, small or large, draw me away from God; let nothing distract, disturb, or hinder me in any way.

Perhaps it is not yet possible for me to arrive at such a point, but everything is possible to God, who, by grace and love, can, within an instant, unite the devout soul to Himself. God's pure and perfect love can, in a moment and as often as it wishes, bring it about that I, with all my past forgotten, become fully inflamed and melt away by the fire of His love.

O my God and my love, when shall I, a pilgrim here, be wholly united to You through all my soul's faculties, which You have graciously given and bestowed on me? Let every creature of Yours be silent before You, my God, and You, who are eternally blessed above all the heavenly stars, alone speak, assist, and enlighten me.

Happy is the soul forsaken by the world but consoled by God; unknown among men but known to the holy angels; ignored by the wicked but appreciated by the godly; despised by the proud but beloved to the humble; dismissed by the worldly but valued by the spiritual; scorned by the mighty but honored by the lowly; externally appearing lifeless but internally thriving; suffering in the flesh but joyful in spirit; weak in body but strong in mind; plain in countenance but beautiful in conscience; worn out by labor but strengthened by prayer; bent over by burdens but erect through consolation; whose body is detained in this world but whose spirit is taken up to heaven and is united to Christ.

Happy is the individual who has Jesus and Mary and all the angels and saints of God as friends in this life, as guides on the way, advisers in doubt, teachers in studies, readers at meals, companions in solitude, associates in conversation, fellow singers in choir, guardians in dangers, attendants in battle, defenders against the enemy, intercessors for sin, assistants at the last hour, consolers during his agony, advocates at judgment, patrons before God, and welcoming friends in heaven.

Pious and devout Brother, now that you have left the world, may God the Father of heaven take the place of your earthly parents; may Jesus be your brother, the Virgin Mary your mother, the angels your friends, and your fellow religious your relatives. May all the faithful be your neighbors, old men your uncles, young men your brothers, married women your mothers, young maidens your sisters, the poor your nephews, and the pilgrims your cousins. May the meek and humble be your close associates, the sober and chaste your table companions, the sick and weak your kindred, the afflicted and oppressed your fellow lodgers, the despised and disdained your acquaintances, all the devout your honored guests, and all who spurn the world and serve Christ your coheirs in the kingdom of heaven.

This is the holy generation and noble progeny born of God, pleasing to God, founded on faith, strengthened by hope, adorned with charity, armed with patience, proved by fire, and constituted in constancy.

30

On True Peace to Be Found in God Alone

Peace be to you! It is I, do not be afraid.
(John 6:20)

Our soul's true peace and only salvation is found in Christ Jesus. Whoever loves Christ enjoys this peace and rests in Him; he need seek nothing more or anything greater.

The faithful soul's peace in this life consists in bearing with much adversity for the love of God and in the name of Christ. He who thinks and judges otherwise is deceived and mistaken. The individual who does not give God first place in all his thinking and doing and who does not desire and sincerely seek Him labors in vain. The Lord says: "There is no peace for the wicked";[1] but there is much peace, Lord, for those who love Your law.

The peace that Christ taught and promised is found in the deepest humility, in the abnegation of our will, in mortifying our depraved desires, in spurning all worldly praise, and in rejecting all outside consolation that comes from what is transitory. Therefore, keep guard over your heart from

[1] Isaiah 57:21.

within and over your senses from without, lest you be ensnared by some allurement harmful to your soul's well-being.

Creatures can often be of help when suitably and properly used to praise the Creator and to honor God and also when used with discretion and moderation for our own needs or for the good of the neighbor. Beautiful objects, on the other hand, when sought after with impassioned and inordinate desire, can often prove harmful, for they can incite the mind to pleasures that are contrary to God's honor and human reason. As the good maintain custody over themselves, the unwary are conquered by their vices!

Wealth indeed tempts, and money corrupts; pleasures poison, and excessive feasting kills; knowledge inflates, power puffs up, and honors lead to pride. Those who are wicked despise the humble, and vain empty praise seduces the fickle-minded. They are senseless fools who strive after such worldly joys and esteem them as great, for in no way are these pleasures capable of satisfying the soul or affording it any rest.

All that is of this world is in itself deficient and short-lived. Outside of God, nothing is perfect, and so nothing, other than He, is to be looked upon as our supreme joy or highest good. Therefore, if you do not want to be deceived or deluded, set not your heart and mind on any living creature, whether of noble birth or handsome in appearance or of stately stature or of high office, because all this is worthless, fleeting, and harmful unless referred to God from whom all good things come and in whom everything lives and has its being.

Therefore, frail and mortal man that you are, give way to no boasting, for you are guilty in many respects, easily prone to evil, and unsteady in virtue; do not place too much confidence in yourself or remain fixed in your opinions about yourself or presume or depend too much on others, but offer and ascribe to God, entirely and without reserve, whatever good you know to be in yourself and in all creatures. It is then that you will find peace and quiet of heart in Christ and not in any created good. That encouraging and holy word of Christ, which he proclaimed on the mount, will then be said of you and fulfilled in you, namely, "Blessed are the clean of heart, for they shall see God."[2]

To Him be praise, honor, and glory from every creature, now and forever. Amen.

[2] Matthew 5:8.

31

On Directing the Right Intention to God

My eyes are ever on the Lord,
for he shall free my feet from the snare.

(*Psalm 25:15*)

In your every thought, word, and deed, always have a right and pure intention directed to God, so that you may accomplish all for the praise, glory, and honor of God and for the edification of the neighbor. Because God is the source of all good merit and the giver of eternal rewards, He ought to be the beginning and end of all your actions; otherwise, you risk losing the fruit of your labor.

If you keep in mind God's dreadful judgments, you will not yield to vanity. Vanity and the desire for everyone's praise is the worst of plagues! Such a desire is certainly pointless, a sure sign of pride, and contrary to God's grace. What then are you to do? And in whom are you to place your confidence and trust? Surely not in yourself or in any man or in anything of this world or in the stars of the heavens, but only in God, your Creator, for it is He who made you and holds you and all creation in His powerful hand—and this without another's help or support.

Therefore, repeat with David as he prays in the Psalms, "My eyes are ever on the Lord, for he shall free my feet from the snare", and again, "Lord, all my desire is before You, and my groaning is not hidden from You."[1] Whatever is your need, ignore the foolish reasoning and counsel of men, and turn confidently to the Lord, your God, with prayers and holy aspirations, for it is He who will free your feet from the snare. Thus you will not be led away from the straight path of virtue and true humility, and you will remain steadfast in God until the very end.

Every good work done for God brings joy to one's conscience, enlightens the mind, and merits an increase in grace; on the other hand, every evil deed brings sadness to the doer, sullies his reputation and obstructs the inflow of divine consolation.

Whoever acts solely out of vanity extinguishes his inner light by the wind of self-affectation, and whoever acts for the sake of the world and to gain its esteem will, because of God's displeasure, fall rather quickly into the mire. Therefore, do not rejoice in any of this world's happiness as does the fool, but stand fast in the fear of God and in the knowledge of your own frailty. Let your frequent lapses and proneness to error teach you to be humble and to have a low opinion of yourself.

[1] Psalm 38:9.

Do not overpraise anyone in this life, because you do not know what the future will bring; neither should you rashly judge anyone who has fallen, because God can quickly raise him up if he repents. Pray for everyone, and commend all to God.

Be vile in your own eyes, that you may be great in the eyes of God, who looks favorably on the humble; from afar He recognizes the proud and immediately casts them behind Him. If men despise you and others are preferred to you, do not give in to too much sadness, because it is safer and better to be humbled along with the meek and simple than to be cast aside by God with the proud and rich.

Be wary of being praised, fear being highly thought of, blush when honored, avoid seeking the esteem of others, and strive to remain hidden. Prefer to spend your time with God in devout prayer and in diligently reading the holy books.

The man who sets aside praise and honor for God is not without praise or honor. Nor is he without divine consolation who views all this world's joys as nothing and willingly endures all that is contrary to him for Christ and longs daily to be with Him in heaven.

32

The Prayer of a Humble and Contrite Heart

*To You, O Lord, who lives in heaven,
I have lifted up my soul.*

(Psalm 25:1)

O Lord God, who wisely and justly orders all things in heaven and on earth—angels, men, and all creatures—I ask You, in place of the praise and thanksgiving that I owe You, to accept the trials and anxieties of my heart, which I now offer in true contrition for my sins. Turn all that is evil in me to good, and what is good to better, and this for the glory of Your name and the eternal salvation of my soul.

You know my every weakness and my frightful ignorance as well as how, because of my wandering mind and erratic memory, I often stray from You, going here and there and at times some distance away from You. According to Your great mercy, Lord, pardon me and delay not in bringing me back to You. Night and day, keep my heart close to You in fervent prayer and holy meditation, as much as is possible for me in this frail body of mine.

My desire is to please Your most loving face with

sacred gifts and prayers, especially with the three mites of the poor, namely: contrition of heart, confession on the lips, and satisfaction through humble works. My Lord God, supremely lovable, remember Your poor servant, for I am a weak-willed man and not a holy angel, a great sinner and not an innocent lamb, one who is lukewarm in prayer and far from fervent in contemplation. Nor am I a worthy servant of Yours; I do not deserve being numbered, seen, or named among those offering You fitting worship.

My dear Lord, in place of the joyful song and jubilation of the angels and the melodious praise of all dwelling in heaven, I ask You to accept my humble prayer and heartfelt contrition for my sins. For my part, I do not despair nor will I despair of ever receiving Your mercy and pardon, though in my frailty I am weighed down and often fall. Neither do I cease now nor will I throughout my life cease praising You; I will praise and magnify You, my God, until my soul finally attains to You. Always to praise You and to love You above all things is the supreme joy of the angels and of the blessed in the eternal homeland.

On Holy Fellowship
with Jesus and His Saints

Seek the Lord, and your soul will live.

(Psalm 69:32)

There is nothing better or anything that makes the soul happier than seeking the Lord. If one were to search for something else, he would find nothing. Therefore, if you desire to have a friend who would be a consolation to you, seek Jesus, either with the shepherds as He lies in the manger or with the holy wise men as He sits in His mother's arms or with Simeon and Anna in the Temple or with Martha at home or with Mary Magdalen at the tomb; or join the Apostles in the Upper Room as they joyfully await the coming of the Holy Spirit.

Blessed is he who, in these and other holy places, devoutly seeks Jesus, not in the body, but in spirit and in truth. Blessed is he who at all times and in all places sincerely seeks Jesus and who earnestly and eagerly longs for and daily prepares for His presence and a clear vision of Him. Blessed is he who during his lifetime follows Jesus in His sufferings and on the Cross, for when his final hour comes all will go well with him and Jesus; he will have no fear of an unfavorable judgment.

Not only should he seek Jesus but also Jesus' disciples as well as all who love Jesus and all who patiently bear with life's adversities for the love of Him. Love of Jesus and His friends leads one to despise the world and to distance oneself from all that is impure and vain.

Leave aside, therefore, your extern friends, acquaintances, and associates, who can be a hindrance to you in your solitude and prayer life, and for your sole consolation seek, in the quiet of your cell, the friendship of the holy Apostles and of Jesus' brethren, that they may speak to you of the kingdom of God and of eternal beatitude and of how, by way of many tribulations, you may arrive in their company.

Before seeking out all the saints and members of the heavenly court, go first to the out-of-the-way home and quiet oratory of the Blessed Virgin Mary, and with insistent prayer seek your soul's consolation there. Listen as the angel of God speaks with Mary about Christ's Incarnation and the redemption of the human race. Oh, happy is the day and blessed the hour if you can remain there listening to the angel Gabriel and the Blessed Virgin Mary as they converse about the heavenly mysteries, and believe most firmly that all that is said by the angel to Mary is true, just as Mary believed God and His angel, sent to her from heaven.

Next, diligently seek our Lord Jesus Christ's precursor, the holy John the Baptist, living hidden in the desert, and on bended knee greet him, asking him most devoutly: "Hail, John, most holy and beloved friend of Jesus, I have heard many good and marvelous things concerning you, about your holy and miraculous birth, how from the time of your youth you lived in strict and holy solitude lest you sin, even slightly, in word or thought."

Ask him how long he remained alone in the desert, and stay with him as long it pleases him and time permits. Learn from him what food he ate and what he drank and who ministered to his needs while he was there. Whether his father and mother sent him anything; did they come to see him, or did he go to visit them? Perhaps the holy angel Gabriel sometimes came down and revealed many secret things to him, and did Jesus personally come and strengthen him as it is written in the Gospel, "For the hand of the Lord was with him"?[1]

Whatever be the answer to all this, commit yourself fully to the Holy Spirit, who taught, filled, and guided John, adorned his entire life with virtues

[1] Luke 1:66.

and guarded over him—in desert, prison, and chains —and at the end of his life received his soul with the martyr's palm.

Then proceed to Christ's Apostles, and seek out Saint Peter, and go with him to the Temple to pray, or else go along with him up to the Upper Room to receive the Holy Spirit. Also look for Paul in Damascus and in Ephesus, and travel with him— not in body but in spirit—wherever he goes to preach the Gospel of Christ. Take note how he labors more than all others, how often he prays, and how frequently during prayer and contemplation he is enraptured and taken up into heaven. Such sublime flights are not granted to all, and after descending to our level, he says, "I do not count myself to have comprehended."[2] And elsewhere, in instructing the humble faithful in the life and sufferings of Christ, he says, "I decided to know nothing among you except Jesus Christ and Him crucified."[3] Follow Saint Paul, and he will lead you along the right path to Christ and by way of the Cross to heaven.

Go farther and seek out the Apostle Andrew, as he preaches Christ in Achaia and its parts, and listen to his words as, in the name of Christ, he hangs on his cross. Inscribe all that he says about Christ's sufferings and his praises of the Holy Cross

[2] Philippians 3:13.

[3] 1 Corinthians 2:2.

on your heart, and strive to fulfill them according to the Holy Spirit's inspiration and assistance.

Then visit Saint James the Greater, who suffered and was killed by Herod, and with him drink the cup of this wretched life's suffering, and patiently endure all sorrows for the love of God and the salvation of your soul.

Then proceed and seek Christ's beloved Apostle John, who was sent into exile in the name of Jesus and was thus separated from all worldly business and affairs. Enlightened by divine revelation from above and using figures and symbols, he wrote the Book of the Apocalypse,[4] in which he speaks of the Church militant and triumphant. After this and last of all, he wrote his Gospel teaching the divinity of Christ, for the instruction and solace of the faithful in all the churches. Read and study these and the other books of Holy Scripture not only for your own betterment but also for your consolation during your time of exile in this world.

For your comfort seek out the other Apostles, all laboring in the service of Christ—edifying many by their words and example and all dying for the faith and the love of Christ. Seek out Saint James, the brother of the Lord, as he writes his canonical epistle, which describes the rule of the Christian life and the perfection of our religion.

[4] This book is more commonly known today as the Book of Revelation.

In India seek Saint Thomas, who reverently touched Christ's wounds, firmly believed, and with burning love unhesitatingly exclaimed: "My Lord and my God!"[5]

Likewise, and with great desire, search out the holy and learned Apostle Matthew the Evangelist, who, while using Hebrew characters, wrote his Gospel of Christ for the benefit of the entire world and the final salvation of all peoples, of all tongues, and of all nations. In the same way and with the same affection, seek out the other Apostles and disciples of Jesus Christ, as they live the word of life in various places, teach the people, and labor in the Lord's vineyard until death.

These, indeed, are the friends and saints of God, who by shedding their blood and wearing the crown of martyrdom have merited eternal life. Read their lives and of their sufferings with great willingness, and you will find consolation in your labors and sorrows, for what you now endure and suffer for Christ in the service of God is as nothing when compared to what the saints and other devout individuals have suffered.

[5] John 20:28.

34

On Placing Our Supreme Good
and Final End in God Alone

I shall be satisfied when Your glory shall appear.

(*Psalm 17:15*)

Lord, how can a man attain to such glory?

By having contempt for oneself and for all things on this earth and by an ardent love for all heavenly goods. In witness to this, we have the souls of all the saints now rejoicing in the heavenly kingdom and all the faithful who strive and struggle against temptations to evil.

Far from ever eternally enjoying this supreme good and glorious end are the proud devils, un-believing pagans, hardened heretics, perverse sin-ners, and carnal men—lovers of the world who never think of God. These place their happiness and final end in earthly goods, worldly honors, and another's praise, and in order to possess, in-crease, and enjoy all these, they scurry about and toil, always on their guard and almost never at rest. Nor do they stop searching until they have acquired their desire, and when they have acquired it, rightly or wrongly, they are still not content but wish to rise still higher and be admired and honored above all others. They parade about thinking themselves wise, considering themselves superior to all and worthy of everyone's homage. What they seek and desire, however, is shallow, trivial, and nothing, and in the long run dangerous and ruinous.

Certainly you are mistaken and deceive yourself thinking that this world is pleasant and the present life pleasurable, for of all that you possess nothing is secure, and, furthermore, day by day you advance nearer to death and God's future judgment. There is nothing in this life so enjoyable that it does not have some admixture of bitterness. Among creatures there is nothing so good, delightful, and wonderful that can satisfy the soul of man and render him totally happy, free him of all that is bad, fill him with all that is good, or grant him endless joy except God our only supreme, eternal, and infinite good. He is the Creator of all that is visible and invisible, of angels and of men; He is before all, above all, and in all; He is God blessed forever.

What can any creature in heaven or on earth possibly say or think that is worthy of God? God surpasses all things, and in His sight all things are vain nothings. Every soul that seeks anything other than God and desires what takes his mind away from God's love and honor is foolish and will forever remain wretched and in dire need.

Lord, great and marvelous are Your works! Neither I nor any creature can possibly understand or comprehend them. What, then, am I to do, who am unable to perceive things far above me or penetrate the secrets of heaven or with the angels contemplate the face of my God? I confess that I am unworthy to enjoy so many benefits and to have converse with the saints in heaven. Hence, as long as I live, I shall always humble and despise myself before God and men; I shall be vile in my own eyes so that God may have mercy on me a sinner, now and always.

With sadness of soul, I will reflect on my past life and on those deeds of mine that deserve Your wrath. By tears and groans I will appease You, God, whom I have often offended in word and deed, by sight, hearing, and by my other senses, all of which You gave me to use, as long as I have this body, in serving You with all my heart.

That I may not yield to despondency or despair because of my past evil deeds I will keep in mind, Lord, all Your goodness and mercies shown me during the past years, until I, with the help of Your grace, merit to attain to salvation.

Free me from all those evils that suddenly and often rush upon me and often distract my heart from thinking about heavenly realities. Dear God, be ever present to me, and place me next to You, lest I begin to stray and distance myself from You, who are my supreme good. You alone, Lord, are all my good; give Yourself to me and satisfy my soul. You alone, Lord, are my salvation. Amen.

~